I0232586

ANSWERING HUMANITY'S COMMON QUESTIONS ABOUT GOD
by Tim Passmore

OUTCOME
PUBLISHING

Answering Humanity's
Common Questions About God
by Tim Passmore

Published by Outcome Publishing
www.gooutcome.com

This book or parts thereof may not be reproduced in any form, stored in a retrieval system, or transmitted in any form by any means – electronic, mechanical, photocopy, recording or otherwise – without prior written permission of the publisher, except as provided by United States of America copyright law.

Scripture excerpts are from the Holy Bible, New International Version (NIV), Copyright 1973, 1978, 1984, 2011 by Biblica Inc. Used by permission. All rights reserved worldwide.

Copyright © 2025 by Tim Passmore

First Edition

Printed in the United States of America

1. Religion: Spirituality General
2. Self-Help: Spiritual
3. Religion: Christian Life – Personal Growth

Table of Contents

READ ME FIRST

I have good news for you. If someone gave you this book, they really care about you. It may have been a risk for them, not knowing how you would respond. For them, it was worth the risk.

They aren't giving you this book because they're judging you. They know they don't have any right to. None of us are perfect. They want you to understand what they have discovered about their own life. They learned it's okay to have questions. All of us have them. It's a part of life's journey. Our questions help us on our search.

What were they searching for? Some call it happiness. They found their true need is joy. They know where it comes from and want you to have it. They believe it's such great news that they can't keep it to themselves. After you've read this, I encourage you to talk to them. They can give you firsthand information about how it has changed their lives.

I hope you enjoy what you are about to read and that it will help you as you decide what to believe about your life. No one can decide that for you. It's your choice. Just know this: no matter what you decide, the person who gave you this book still cares about you and wants the best for you.

1

WHAT ARE YOU THINKING?

If we were meeting in person, I'd say "Hi! I'm Tim. What your name?" and shake your hand.
But we're not meeting in person. Although I'd prefer to have a conversation with you, that's not possible in this one-way format.

So instead I'll answer questions that I assume you're asking. I can easily assume you have them because some questions are common—all humans want them answered. Those answers help us make decisions about our belief or nonbelief in the existence of God and our need for him.

I'll begin by asking you a question that comes from another assumption—that you may be thinking about God. I don't think this is too far of a stretch, knowing that someone may have given you this book, understanding you may be thinking about God. Or maybe the title of the book drew your attention. For whatever reason, you may be thinking about him.

The question is, what are you thinking?

I ask because it's important to understand why we are thinking about God. Obviously, I don't know why you may be thinking about him. There are several reasons people do. Many don't think about him until they are in an uncontrollable situation and need help no person can give. They need help from someone more powerful than we are. They need their circumstances to change, and they know it can happen in only one way. They need God!

Maybe you are struggling with your sense of self and are feeling low because you feel like something is missing. People who observe you from the outside would say that you have everything: a good job, a safe place to live, and material possessions that add value to your personal life. There is one problem—you don't feel happy. You might be thinking there must be something more—and the more might be God.

Maybe you are looking at what is happening in our world and thinking about the evil behavior of people. You notice how they abuse and use one another, resulting in division, harm, and destruction. What would change this? You may be asking questions like these:

- *If there is a God, why would he allow our world to become so unhealthy?*
- *If there is a God, could he be the solution to the mess our world is in?*
- *If there is a God who could make a difference, how does he want me to live to help solve our challenges?*

Maybe you are getting older and beginning to think about what happens to you after you die. You may be asking questions like these:

- *Is our earthly existence all there is, or is there another life for me after I'm gone?*
- *Is there life after death?*
- *I know there is an earth, but is there a heaven?*
- *If there is a heaven, how do I get there?*

WHY WE DON'T BELIEVE IN GOD

According to a 2022 Gallup polling article, when participants were asked "Do you believe in God?", 81 percent of respondents said yes. This compares to 92 percent who responded in the same way in 2011. This survey reveals two important facts. First, the majority of people believe in God. Second, the number of people who believe in God is declining.[1]

Why is the number of people declining?

That's a great question! A logical answer is that people don't believe they need him. They are finding meaning for their lives in something other than God. As long as they feel good and as long as what they live for gives them what they need, they won't choose to know him. Why would they?

Those who choose God do so because they have determined that what they've trusted for happiness and to meet their needs doesn't work. They are looking for someone who does.

Maybe this is you.

There is another answer to the question. Some don't believe in him because they believe he's judgmental.

They believe that he is against them because of their behavior. As humans, we long to be accepted and not judged. We feel unsettled when we're judged, and many will do what they can to avoid it. One solution is to associate with people who agree with our philosophy of life. We connect with those who believe that what we live for brings meaning and happiness. We do this because we believe we know what is best.

Do we know what is best? If we do, we will not feel a need for God. If we don't, we understand our need for him. Believing in a God who knows what is best poses a challenge for us.

Let's make it personal. We may say, "What if I'm living for something that God knows is not best for me? If I am, I don't want to feel judged!" This also may be you.

We've learned that this is a common feeling. It may be keeping you from wanting to know him. We need a different approach.

CHANGING MINDSETS

We can think about judgment in a different way. What we see as a negative is really a positive.
If there is a God, certainly this God must make judgments about what is best. We would expect him to do this, especially if he wants what is best for us. He must make a judgment and communicate it to us. He would want us

to make course changes when the direction we are going leads to harm and heartache. If he wants us to live a great life, he must tell us when we are on a path that leads away from experiencing it.

Where many see this judgment as a bad thing, God's guidance is meant to be helpful.

What does that mean?

He's not against us, he's for us! He wants the best for us. He loves us and is bothered when he sees those he created missing out on their best life. He wants to help them find it!

Why does God know best?

He created us. He's the inventor. He knows how we're put together and the purpose for our being made. There is another reason. He knows what's best because he has more knowledge.

Our mindset about God also begins to change when we understand that what we know is limited, while his knowledge far exceeds our own. We are limited by our knowledge of what has happened in the past and what is happening in the present. We don't know the future.

What if there is a God who is not bound by these limits? What if there is a God who knows the past, present and the future? Why would I choose to trust in my limited perspective when I could trust in the one who has more knowledge and more understanding of how circumstances are working together to accomplish something that I don't yet see?

A DESIRE FOR JOY

I want to help those who are searching for God find the truth about him. We need to know who God really is and not who people make him out to be. He's not some cosmic killjoy who is trying to make our lives miserable; he is the one who wants us to experience joy. He created us for this purpose. He wants us to live with it no matter what may be happening to us or around us.

There is a difference between happiness and joy. Happiness is a temporary feeling that things are good. Because it's temporary, happiness goes away. This leads us to search for something more to help us feel good again. What we've trusted in doesn't satisfy.

What are we looking for?

We're looking for joy. It's different. Joy can be permanent. It can go on without coming to an end. Joy, like happiness, is a good feeling. However, it comes from something that we have that cannot be taken away, no matter what. No bad circumstance or event affects it.

Where does joy come from?

It comes from a relationship with someone who loves us even when we do unloving things. We're loved even when we make mistakes and fail. It's a love that isn't dependent on our moral condition, doing right or wrong. It's an unconditional love that never ends.

Why is this important?

We all have the same need. We all need to be loved. It's the reason why many lose their happiness. What they trust in to feel good doesn't give them the love they're looking for.

The relationship that brings joy is the relationship that many believe God wants to have with us. I'm one who believes this to be true. He loves us unconditionally and wants us to be a part of His family. It's a relationship that can't be taken away.

This is great news! Our lives can have value and meaning in all circumstances. We have reasons to be here. I exist to have a loving relationship with God and to show God's love to others, helping them have the joy that I found in knowing him.

If someone gave you this book, that's what they're hoping for you. They believe this news is too good to keep to themselves. They believe that a relationship with God can be the answer you've been looking for.

PERSONAL EXPERIENCE, SCIENCE, AND HISTORY

I want to share with you what I've learned and help you make your decision of what to believe about God.

I've also been skeptical about God. Although I grew up in the home of a Baptist pastor, as I began to form my own beliefs, I had questions. I consider myself to be somewhat intelligent. After all, I went "all the way" in school, earning a doctoral degree. I don't write this to brag. I say this to help you understand the perspective from which I come. I'm not a person who just takes someone's word in what they say. I want to know if it's true. I've been searching for what is true. Because of this, I've had several personal experiences of learning information that have helped answer my questions. I've been exposed to some smart people in areas of study that affect our human condition.

As for science, we'll learn what some popular scientists have said that help us as we draw our conclusions about the existence or nonexistence of God.

We'll also look to a historical record of people's belief in God. The historical record we'll be looking at is known as the Bible. Before you freak out and say, "But I don't believe in the Bible," let me explain the context in which we'll use it. I get that some don't believe what many Christians believe about the Bible. Many of us believe it was inspired by God in its writing and therefore is His Word to humanity. I know that's a real stretch for some who don't believe in God. I'm not trying to convince you of that.

I want to encourage you to think about the Bible the way most people, whether they believe in God or not, can think about it. It's a historical document. This is fact. It was written many years ago to document the beliefs that people had about God during the times of its writing. It tells us about historical events and gives perspective from those who believed in him.

If we are going to make a decision about our belief in God or our understanding of him, we need to know what people have said about him. This will help us answer our questions.

2

What Do I Want To Know?

Every person has common fundamental questions. There are four that we all want answered.

THE FUNDAMENTAL QUESTIONS

The Origin Question: Where did we come from? Is there a God, or did the universe always exist? If there is a God, we want to know what he is like. We want to know if we can connect with him and have a relationship with him. If we can, we want to know how this happens. If there is a God, he helps us answer the other questions. If there is no God, we rely on ourselves to answer them.

The Morality Question: What is right and wrong behavior? If there is a God, he determines right from wrong. He created us to feel when something is correct or incorrect. If there is no God, we define what is right and wrong. People's behaviors are important because they show how others feel about us. For example, we all desire love. If someone loves us, they should treat us right. If someone doesn't love us, they treat us wrong. These are the measurements we use to determine whether someone really cares.

The Destiny Question: Is there life after death? Not only do we desire love, but we also desire eternity. We long for something beyond this life. We don't want this to be the end of us. We wonder if there is something more. If there is life after death, what is it like? How do I experience it? If it is through God, how can I come to know him?

The Meaning Question: What is my purpose in life? Not only do we desire love and eternity, but we also desire significance. We want to feel good about what we are doing. If there is a God, he determines how we find purpose. If there is no God, we decide for ourselves. God's purpose for us is to show His love to others—to do what is right for them. We show the type of love to others that we desire. This gives us joy. Our purpose without God is to do what makes us happy. We use whatever means necessary to gain it. We may believe that happiness comes through physical pleasure, personal power, social connections or personal possessions.

Now that we know the questions, let's take a look at a historical account and learn that these questions are nothing new. The event happened during Biblical times and shows us how people responded to the message about God and Jesus, the one Christians believe to be the Son of God.

THE SKEPTICS

A guy named Paul had an encounter with Jesus and became one of his followers. He was spreading the message about Jesus and his love for others. People of his day were asking the same questions we ask today. He shared that Jesus was the answer they were looking for.

Even if you are not a Christian, you have most likely heard about Jesus dying on the cross and the claim that Jesus came back to life. This is called the resurrection. After the crucifixion and resurrection occurred, the message spread about what had happened, and people wanted to know if it was true.

Paul taught them about Jesus and did it by telling them his own personal experience. There were no scriptures about Jesus's life at that time. They were still being written. Not having this available to him, he told others what had happened to him and reasoned with them about why they could also come to believe in God.

On one occasion, while Paul was in Athens waiting for Silas and Timothy (two other followers of Jesus), a group of Epicureans and Stoic philosophers came to hear Paul talk about Jesus. After he spoke, they invited him to come with them to a place called the Areopagus. It was a location where the leaders and deep thinkers in the community would gather to discuss current events. We read:

> *While Paul was waiting for them in Athens, he was greatly distressed to see that the city was full of idols. So he reasoned in the synagogue with both Jews and God-fearing Greeks, as well as in the marketplace day by day with those who happened to be there. A group of Epicurean and Stoic philosophers began to debate with him. Some of them asked, "What is this babbler trying to say?" Others remarked, "He seems to be advocating foreign gods." They said this because Paul was preaching the good news about Jesus and the resurrection. Then they took him and brought him to a meeting of the Areopagus, where they said to him, "May we know what this new teaching is that you are presenting? You are bringing some strange ideas to our ears, and we would like to know what they*

mean." (All the Athenians and the foreigners who lived there spent their time doing nothing but talking about and listening to the latest ideas.)

Paul then stood up in the meeting of the Areopagus and said: "People of Athens! I see that in every way you are very religious. For as I walked around and looked carefully at your objects of worship, I even found an altar with this inscription: to an unknown god. So you are ignorant of the very thing you worship— and this is what I am going to proclaim to you.

"The God who made the world and everything in it is the Lord of heaven and earth and does not live in temples built by human hands. And he is not served by human hands, as if he needed anything. Rather, he himself gives everyone life and breath and everything else. From one man he made all the nations, that they should inhabit the whole earth; and he marked out their appointed times in history and the boundaries of their lands. God did this so that they would seek him and perhaps reach out for him and find him, though he is not far from any one of us. 'For in him we live and move and have our being.' As some of your own poets have said, 'We are his offspring.'

"Therefore since we are God's offspring,

we should not think that the divine being is like gold or silver or stone—an image made by human design and skill. In the past God overlooked such ignorance, but now he commands all people everywhere to repent. For he has set a day when he will judge the world with justice by the man he has appointed. He has given proof of this to everyone by raising him from the dead."

When they heard about the resurrection of the dead, some of them sneered, but others said, "We want to hear you again on this subject." At that, Paul left the Council. Some of the people became followers of Paul and believed. Among them was Dionysius, a member of the Areopagus, also a woman named Damaris, and a number of others. (Acts 17:16–34)

Notice that this event begins by explaining to us that Paul reasoned with the people. Paul understood the importance of unlocking their minds to the idea of God and of Jesus being our way to God. There were those who were close-minded to any other way of life than the one they had chosen for themselves. He knew he needed to help them think about God in a new way.

Who were these guys, the Epicureans and Stoics, who invited him to go to the Areopagus? The Epicureans followed the belief called Epicureanism, the philosophical doctrine of Epicurus, an ancient Greek philosopher. Epicurus held that the highest good is pleasure, which can be experienced through indulgence. It was the "if it feels good do it" philosophy.

Then there were the Stoics. This school of philosophy was founded by Zeno, another Greek philosopher, who taught that people should be free from passion, unmoved by joy or grief, and submitting without complaint to the circumstances of life. The belief of the Stoics was in their ability to maintain self-control and to need no one else. Only through the discipline of their thought could they keep themselves from passion and be unmoved by joy or grief. They did this to protect themselves from being controlled by the circumstances of life.

These groups followed two extremely different paths, yet both still had questions. Why? Could it be that their philosophical beliefs didn't give them what they were looking for? Did their beliefs leave them feeling hopeless, like there must be something more?

This would make sense. Here's why. These philosophies don't provide what we desire in life. Remember, we're looking for joy that does not end. The Epicureans' belief in pleasure falls short because pleasure ends and we're looking for more. What they hoped would be the source of meaning in life didn't provide it. The Epicurean philosophy doesn't give us what we desire.

We also discover that we can't handle every situation in life like the Stoics believed. Our hope of getting through difficulty is dashed when we face more than we can handle. Some things are out of our control, and it's difficult for these circumstances not to affect our emotions. It leads to our feeling of hopelessness.

We try both philosophies, but they fall short. These realities about pleasure and self-effort could very well be the reason why they were curious to learn about Jesus and how he connects us to God. They must have been looking for something that only God could provide. They needed to have hope in someone that would satisfy us in every situation of life.

Even the people whom Paul was interacting with at this place, some of the most intellectual of their day, were searching for God. We know this to be true because of this historical account. They had a name for God. They called him "The Unknown God." He was important to them; they swore in the name of the Unknown God when making agreements with one another.

Paul acknowledged their belief in this God. We read this in the historical account. *"Paul then stood up in the meeting of the Areopagus and said: 'People of Athens! I see that in every way you are very religious. For as I walked around and looked carefully at your objects of worship, I even found an altar with this inscription: to an unknown god.'" (Acts 17:22–23)*

Paul then told them who God is. *" 'For in him we live and move and have our being.' As some of your own poets have said, 'We are his offspring.' Therefore since we are God's offspring, we should not think that the divine being is like gold or silver or stone—an image made by human design and skill." (Acts 17:28–29)*

If he is not gold, silver or stone, then who is he? He's the God who created us. He's the God that we can know personally. He's also the God who meets our desires for love, eternity and significance.

The most important of these is the desire for love. God is a God of love, and we need him. The difference in their image of the Unknown God made of gold, silver, and stone and the God who created us is that gold, silver, and stone don't love us back.

We're looking for someone to love us back!

We're looking for someone to love us in a specific way. We need someone who loves us no matter what we're like and no matter what we've done. We need someone to love us unconditionally. This doesn't mean that we need a God who supports our being who we want to be or our doing what we want to do if we're not living up to His desires. We need a God who loves us even when we fall short. He loves us enough to do what is necessary to help us become who he created us to be so we can find joy.

What does this love look like?

We need someone who shows us. Paul told them about the one who had come to be the example of God's love. His name is Jesus. He showed his love to everyone, even to those considered to be the worst of their day, like prostitutes and thieves. He didn't shun them or condemn them; he spent time with them, pointed out where they had messed up, offered them forgiveness for what they had done out of his concern and compassion for them, and encouraged them to be better. He encouraged them to turn from their selfish life and to become selfless by loving God and those he created.

There is a word for our turning from selfishness to selflessness. We read it in the historical account above. The word is *repent*. This is an old military term which means to do an about-face. We're going in one direction, and we turn completely around and go in the opposite direction. God leads us to do this.

When we love him more than all else, we turn from a life of living for what we want to living a life for what he desires. His desire is for us to show his love for those he has created. We do this through service, even if it means we need to sacrifice for their good. That's what Jesus did for us.

It was through Jesus's service to those who were living self-centered lives and his service to those who were in need that people saw what God's love looks like. We see God's love through people. Jesus was the greatest example of this love. Why? He did something for everyone.

Paul told the people about Jesus's death on the cross and his coming back to life. They needed to know why Jesus did it.

He died to take the punishment for their selfish behavior so they didn't have to. God resurrected Jesus and brought him back to life to give us hope that if we accept what Jesus did for us by dying for our selfish behavior, we could also come back to life after our death and live with God forever in heaven.   This gives us the hope we're looking for. We have hope for a great future with him. Their feeling of hopelessness could be overcome by accepting the loving sacrifice Jesus made for them. He was the answer they were looking for!

Paul told them about Jesus, and they responded to what he had said. They didn't all respond the same way. *"When they heard about the resurrection of the dead, some of them sneered, but others said, 'We want to hear you again on this subject.' At that, Paul left the Council. Some of the people became followers of Paul and believed. Among them was Dionysius, a member of the Areopagus, also a woman named Damaris, and a number of others." (Acts 17:32–34)*

Some rejected him outright. To them, if they didn't see it, touch it, or experience it firsthand, they couldn't logically accept it. They sneered! They didn't have faith that what they were hearing about Jesus was true.

Some wanted to think about it more and were considering it. A number of them believed.

The same is true today. These are the responses that people have toward accepting the message of Jesus. Some don't believe it because they can't trust what they have heard. They rely on logic and choose not to have faith. Some are considering that it might be true, but they need more reason to place their faith in Jesus. Others believe what they hear about Jesus, know he is the way to have a relationship with the God and accept what he did on the cross and through his resurrection so they can be forgiven for what they've done wrong and become a part of God's family forever.

HOW WE RESPOND TO WHAT WE HEAR ABOUT JESUS

Have you heard about Jesus? If you have, how have you responded to him? Let me ask you some questions:

If you don't believe in what Jesus did to show his love for you through his death and resurrection, what would it take for you to believe?

If you are considering placing faith in what Jesus did for you, what is holding you back from making that decision?

If you do believe in Jesus and have placed your faith in what he did for you, why did you do it? The reason you made the decision to trust in Jesus may be helpful to others who have not yet chosen to place their faith in him.

Don't gloss over these questions too quickly. Try grabbing a journal or notepad and write down your answers. If you're struggling with the answers, or with how to use your answers to help others, talk to the person who gave you this book. They want to help.

WHAT CHANGES OUR RESPONSE TO JESUS

Paul shared this message with people in multiple cities, including Athens, for a reason. He had met Jesus. Paul had been a big-time skeptic! He was very religious and had been trained by a great Jewish teacher. He lived to protect Judaism and at first saw Jesus as a threat to their religion.

He didn't believe what Jesus's followers were saying about him. They were saying he was the Messiah. They were saying Jesus was the way to God. They were even referred to as people of "The Way."

Paul didn't believe this and used his authority as a Jewish leader to have the people of "The Way" (Christians) put to death.

One day Paul was traveling on the road to Damascus, and he encountered Jesus, who had already died and been resurrected. Jesus appeared to Paul (known as Saul at the time) in the form of a bright light. The light was so bright that it blinded him (Acts 9:8). Jesus asked him, "why do you persecute me?" (Acts 9:4) He had been persecuting Jesus by having his followers put to death. Although Jesus could have left him in this blind condition, he didn't. Paul obviously deserved it. Instead, Jesus offered something Paul didn't deserve. He offered to heal him.

Get the picture! Paul is in a situation that he can do nothing about. He's blind and can't heal himself. He needs a miracle. He needs Jesus to heal him. He no longer can rely on his own ability to provide what he needs for himself; he needs someone more powerful than him or any human being.

Jesus sends him to a guy's house, and through him works a miracle. Paul is healed. Jesus not only heals him, he forgives him for what he had done.

This event changed Paul's life. He knew he had done wrong. He was blown away that the one he was doing it against didn't hold a grudge against him or want to harm him. He wanted him to be healed and forgiven.

Paul had been living for something that did not give him joy. It couldn't. We can't feel good when we treat others in a way we don't want to be treated. It's the Golden Rule. Do you know who gave it to us? It was Jesus! He said, *"Do to others as you would have them do to you (Luke 6:31)."*

Now Paul found joy! He began a relationship with God as a member of his family and wanted as many people as possible to have what he had. He wanted them to be saved from a joyless life.

Paul would later write a letter to some Christians living in the city of Corinth. He told them his purpose. *"To the weak I became weak, to win the weak. I have become all things to all people so that by all possible means I might save some. I do all this for the sake of the gospel, that I may share in its blessings. (1 Corinthians 9:22–23)*

What does this mean? Paul put himself in the place of the person who had a weakness to understand their struggle and to give them the answer for it. The answer is the gospel.

I know, that sounds very churchy. You may have heard someone say "the gospel truth," because in the church we accept the gospels as true historical accounts. The word gospel means good news, but to those who believe, it also implies truth.

What truth did Paul share? He shared the truth that God loves the imperfect. He shared the truth that God desires to forgive those who are not perfect and provided a way by sending Jesus to die for their selfish behavior. He shared the truth that God wants to have a relationship with us even though we've been imperfect. He wants us in the family. That's great news!

Paul could relate. He was weak and needed God's help. We're all weak and need God's help.

This is the reason for this book. I want to do what Paul was doing. I want to help those who have weaknesses. I can relate. I have them. I also want to help those who don't believe in Jesus to understand why those who do believe in him can do so with confidence. I want to help you deal with the doubts you may have that are keeping you from making the decision to join God's family.

Let's get back to the Epicureans and Stoics. What made the difference in how Paul's listeners responded? Some could only use their heads to make decisions. Others were able to use their heads and their hearts. God speaks to us through both.

I can't make anyone believe in God. I can't reason people to God. I can help people reason why the idea of the existence of God is plausible and makes sense. I also can't change someone's heart. I can't make someone feel confident that what they are hearing is true.

If you feel it's true, that's not me speaking to you, it's God. This confidence comes from him. When we believe it's true in our hearts, we can place our faith in him. We trust that God knows what's best.

Faith is important. This is demonstrated through the life of a guy named Richard Wurmbrand, a Romanian of Jewish descent who became an evangelical pastor. He is called "the voice of the underground church." From the late 1940s to the 1960s he was repeatedly jailed and tortured for a total of fourteen years.[2]

One day one of his captors, an atheist, asked him (in a not so kind way) how long he would continue to keep his "stupid religion."

He answered, "I have seen innumerable atheists regretting on their deathbeds that they have been godless; they called on Christ. Can you imagine that a Christian could regret when death is near that he has been a Christian and call on Marx or Lenin to rescue him from his faith?"

The officer laughed and told him it was a clever answer. Then Richard continued with an illustration.

When an engineer has built a bridge, the fact that a cat can pass over the bridge is no proof that the bridge is good. A train must pass over it to prove its strength.

The fact that you can be an atheist when everything goes well does not prove the truth of atheism. It does not hold up in moments of great crisis.

I used Lenin's books to prove to him that, even after becoming prime minister of the Soviet Union, Lenin himself prayed when things went wrong.[3]

Life was cool for Paul until there was a crisis that he could not solve without Jesus. The solution was trusting

Jesus to do what he couldn't do for himself which gave him what he was really looking for.

Again, I'll ask the question posed in the first chapter. What are you thinking? Why are you thinking about God?

3

HOW DO I DECIDE WHAT TO BELIEVE?

We're in a search for truth.
We want to know what is true and what is false. How do I decide what to believe? This is an important question. Why? What we believe to be true guides our choices throughout life. Our beliefs become the filters that we use when deciding what we say and what we do.

To answer this question, we need to know what is involved in our decision-making.

THE TWO PATHS TO DISCOVERING TRUTH

There are two paths we can take to discover what is true. Our search for truth happens by understanding both the physical and the spiritual. Karen Henley is an author who helps skeptical people understand the existence of God and our need for him. In her book *Love Trumps Karma,* she helps us understand the difference between these truths.[4]

Physical Truth
This is determined through the physical world. Physical truth is found by scientifically looking at physical elements in the natural world to come to conclusions. We look at physical evidence and decide on the best explanation for what we discover. We believe something because the physical evidence leads us to believe it.

Spiritual Truth
We may make a statement like "I feel it's true in my Spirit." What does that mean? Spiritual truth is made up of our gut-level feelings. We all have them. I'll give you an example of this. It's called morality. We know the difference between right and wrong without someone telling us this. We know something is right when we treat others the way we want to be treated and we know

something is wrong when we don't. It's why we know that rape, murder, stealing, lying and other hurtful behaviors are wrong behaviors. Our spirit, our gut, tells us this. Just as we have a spiritual, or gut feeling, that something is right or wrong, we also have a spiritual gut feeling that something is true or false. It even happens in the scientific world. A scientist has a hunch, a gut-level feeling about something, and then works to prove his or her theory through physical facts. It began with an inward belief that something was true. The Greeks had a word for this, *splanchnon,* which means intestines or guts.[5] Another word for this is our spirit.

We combine the physical with the spiritual to discover truth. We use these two forms of truth to form our beliefs. This leads to another factor which helps in the forming of what we believe.

THE ROLE THAT LOGIC PLAYS IN BELIEF

We've learned that the first fundamental question is the Origin Question: Where did I come from? Is there a God who created us or did we come into existence in some other way?

We are trying to determine if there is a God. How do we decide this? How can I come to believe he really exists? After all, I can't physically see him. Something is required to believe in God. It's faith! Faith is trusting in what we do not see. In this case, trusting in a God that we do not see. Why would we do this? Let's consider the different types of faith. There are two.

Blind Faith. This faith says, "I'll believe you just because you say it's true." There is no need for evidence. It's childlike faith. At early stages of a child's development, they believe that what their parents say is true. Then things change. They become teenagers. They begin questioning whether what their parents say is true. This moves them into a different type of faith.

Reasoned Faith. This faith says, "I'll believe something because the evidence points to it being the best explanation." We decide what to believe through logical reasoning. Most rely on reasoned faith when deciding what to believe. This gets back to something we've already learned. We reason using physical evidence supported through a gut-level (spirit) feeling that it is true.

We use truth and logic to form our beliefs. Let's get back to the question "Is there a God?" Can we conclude, using physical and spiritual truths and logic, that there is a God? Can we be rational and believe this? Can an intelligent person decide that there is a God?

Why do we come to different conclusions?

Some look around, see the circumstances of life and say, "There must not be a God." Why do they believe this?

Because God doesn't do what they would do if they were God. So they reason "There must not be a God."

Think about what is involved in this reasoning. To feel this way—that God doesn't do what we would do if we were God—is to assume that we are as good as God and know as much as him and therefore can make the decisions that God should be making.

If there is a God, hopefully he is better than we are. We are corrupted through others who influence us to think only of ourselves. We become selfish.

If God created us, it makes common sense that he would want to protect and care for those he has created. He wants the best for us. He is thinking about helping us and we are thinking only of helping ourselves. We should be like him, caring for others, but we have been corrupted. My motive can be selfish while his motive is selfless.

For us to say that we are as qualified to make decisions as God assumes that we are not corrupted, as God is not corrupted, and therefore have nothing to cloud our thinking about what God should do in our world. I have a suspicion that not many people believe this to be true. If there is a God, we can understand that we are imperfect and he is more perfect than we are. He is better than us! If he wasn't, why would we want to know him? Why would we want a relationship with someone selfish? We wouldn't!

We also recognize that if there is a God, that we don't know as much as he does. As we've already learned, he knows the past, present, and future and knows how what is happening today fits into the big picture. Our knowledge is limited to the past and the present which keeps us from being qualified to make the best decisions.

Unfortunately, some people see God in the wrong way. This reminds me of the illustration of an image which can be seen in one of two ways. Susan Barrett shared this image in her book *It's All in Your Head.* It's a common image. Maybe you've seen it before.[6]

What do you see when you look at the image?

Do you see the vase? Why? Is it because I told you there is a vase? Did I influence you to look for a vase? Is there something else that you could see? Some see a vase and others see two people looking at each other. The image hasn't changed. The difference is in how we see the image or what we're looking for when we look at the image.

This connects well with how we see God. God hasn't changed. Our problem is we have changed God into who we think he should be. We want him to live up to our expectations. We see him in only one way because we have seen him that way all along.

Susan Barrett made a key point. If this is the first time you have seen the image, you may be able to easily go back and forth and see both possibilities: the vase and two faces. What happens if you have only seen this in one way for a long time? It becomes more difficult to see the other image even though it's there.[7]

The difficulty with God for some is in how they see him. They've only seen him in one way for a long time. Their opinion about him makes it difficult for them to change their view. I'll give you an example of this.

DEALING WITH EVIL IN THE WORLD

Many struggle with God's existence because of the presence of evil in the world. One of my favorite authors who uses logic and reasoning to conclude that there is a God is Lee Strobel. He's written many helpful books, including *The Case for Christ* and *The Case for Faith*.

He was a skeptic who came to believe in God and to see his need for the work of Jesus on the cross and through his resurrection.

Lee was a reporter in Chicago. He was an atheist whose wife became a Christian, and he had a difficult time dealing with it. He decided to do investigative research as a journalist to come to his own conclusion. His books chronicle the interviews he had with many intelligent people who helped him come to his conclusions.

In *The Case for Faith*, he highlights what David Hume, a famous skeptic, said: "It's just barely possible that God exists."[8] Hume recognized that the existence of God is possible. He struggled with the presence of evil in the world. He acknowledged that our perspective about God makes a difference. He went on to say, "How can a mere finite human be sure that infinite wisdom would not tolerate certain short-range evils in order for more long-range goods that we couldn't foresee?"[9] He brings out the possibility that somehow evil plays a role in the world.

Do you remember the story about the Epicureans, Stoics, and Paul? Listen to what Epicurus, the philosopher, taught: "Either God wants to abolish evil, and cannot; or he can, but does not want to; or he cannot and does not want to. If he wants to but cannot, he is impotent. If he can, and does not want to, he is wicked. But, if God both can and wants to abolish evil, then how comes evil in the world?"[10]

That's a great question! What's the answer? Strobel pointed out what Peter Kreeft, a professor of philosophy at Boston College, said about this topic. When asked if God was creator of evil, he responded, "No…The source of evil is not God's power but mankind's freedom."[11]

One person blames God. That's their opinion of God. That's the image they have of him. The other person knows that our own choices have led us down the difficult path we find ourselves on. They see God in a completely different way.

THERE IS AN EXPLANATION FOR EVIL IN THE WORLD

Henley told a story about a conversation between a missionary named Ken Rideout and someone who was very skeptical about God. Allow me to paraphrase. He was having lunch with an Indonesian banker when the banker said to him, "I have lived a long time and have seen lots of evil in this world: killing, war, injustice, cruelty. In fact, right outside the door of this restaurant, there are people who don't have enough food to eat, and here we sit in luxury enjoying ourselves. If there were a God, he would not create or tolerate a world like this. Therefore, I don't believe there's a God. If there were a God, he would not be worthy of my respect."

After hearing this, Ken took out a piece of paper and drew a line down the middle, making two columns. On the left, he wrote The World. Then he listed the evils for which the banker had accused God.

THE WORLD
Lying
Cheating
Stealing
Adultery
Rape
Murder
War
Cruelty

On the other side, he wrote "God." Pointing to the chart, Ken repeated what the banker had just said, blaming God for allowing these terrible situations to exist in the world such as adultery, lying cheating, murder, stealing, rape, war, and cruelty.

THE WORLD   **GOD**
Lying
Cheating
Stealing
Adultery
Rape
Murder
War
Cruelty

"Let's say that there is no God," said Ken. He drew an X through God's name in the right column.

THE WORLD
Lying
Cheating
Stealing
Adultery
Rape
Murder
War
Cruelty

G⨯D

"Has anything changed now that we have taken God out of the picture?" "No," said the banker. "Without God in the picture, who is to blame for the evil that is in the world: the lying stealing, cheating, murder, adultery, rape, war, and so forth?" asked Ken. "People," said the banker. Ken wrote "people" in the right column under the crossed-out "God."

THE WORLD
Lying
Cheating
Stealing
Adultery
Rape
Murder
War
Cruelty

G⨯D

PEOPLE

Why blame people for all of the evil?" Ken asked. "The tiger eats the deer. The cat eats the mouse. A landslide wipes out an entire village. Why don't we blame the tiger, cat, and landslide in the same way we blame people?" "Because people are responsible beings with wills," said the banker. "People choose their actions." "Are you sure people are responsible?" Ken asked. "Yes," said the banker. "Then why blame God for what you say people have freely chosen to do?" asked Ken. "If people are responsible for choosing to do evil, we might as well put God back in the picture. It seems like God may be people's only hope to get out of the mess they've made of life."[12]

Many have looked at the evidence and come to different conclusions about the existence of God, and if there is a God, what he is like. As people have been considering the existence of God, several worldviews have come into being. In fact, the major beliefs that we find in the world are associated with these worldviews. Let's take a look at them.

THE WORLDVIEWS

Naturalism/Materialism. The belief that the universe (or nature) has always been in existence. Because the universe has always been, there is no need for a God to begin it. Atheists fall within this worldview. They believe there is no God. They believe in the natural world (what we can see, hear, touch, smell, and taste) and discard the possibility of a spiritual world (the existence of a presence that is separate from nature, more powerful than nature and that can create nature).

Pantheism. The belief that God is in all things. I am God and you are God and the essence of God is in all things of nature. They emphasize the protection of people and the environment. To destroy anything in nature is to destroy God. Those who fall within this worldview include Hindus, Buddhists, Taoists, and members of other eastern religions.

Deism. The belief that there is a God who created the universe, but he is impersonal and we cannot have a relationship with him. The Greek religions fall within this worldview. For example, Zeus is the god who created the world.

Theism. The belief that there is a God who created the universe and that he is personal and that we can have a relationship with him. Those who are Christian, Jewish, and Islamic fall within this worldview.

Agnosticism. The belief that there may or may not be a God. Agnostics don't know if there is a God and believe that it is impossible to have any knowledge of things beyond the physical realm.

Which of these worldviews is the best explanation? We need to look at the evidence to answer this question.

Where do we go from here? To determine what we believe, using truth and logic, we need to consider the four fundamental questions in more detail.

4

WHERE DID WE COME FROM?

Where do you believe we came from? What are the possibilities?

THE ORIGIN QUESTION

We were either created by a god or we came into existence in some other natural way. Why do I say natural way? There is a difference between the natural and the supernatural. Nature is all physical things, from the smallest of cells to the largest of animals. It's the water that beats against the shore and the mountain that stretches high into the sky. It's what we see, touch, smell, hear, and taste. Nature can be studied and examined and encountered because of its physical nature.

The supernatural is separate from nature. The word supernatural comes from two words, super and nature. It represents something more powerful than nature that can create and control nature.

Nature does not create. It changes, but it does not bring something into existence that did not previously exist. Things may exist in new forms, but they are made of something previously present.

The word made is important. If there is a supernatural force, this force can create. It can make something new that did not exist in any form before.

Now we see the difference between the beliefs with more clarity. Who is right?

What does the evidence say about where the natural world came from? Does it prove that the universe (nature) has always existed, revealing that there is no need for a God? Or does it prove that there was a beginning point to the universe? If so, there must be another force that caused it to begin. This force is separate from nature and can create it. The force is a supernatural being.

If the physical evidence is inconclusive, what does the spiritual evidence (our gut-level feeling) tell us is the best explanation?

WAS THERE A BEGINNING POINT?

We must decide if there was a starting point to the universe. Was there a point when time began?

If there was a beginning point, there must be something or someone who brought it into existence. There was nothing, but then there was something. Who created that something? What does the evidence reveal?

Edwin Hubble. Let's consider the discoveries of Edwin Hubble. This name may sound familiar to you, because he is the namesake of the Hubble Space Telescope, which is used to look deep into the universe. Hubble was an American astronomer who played an important role in the fields of extragalactic astronomy and observational cosmology. He proved that many objects which were previously thought to be clouds of dust and gas were actually galaxies beyond the Milky Way. He found that there are many galaxies and that these galaxies are expanding outward.[13] This is a scientific fact that we have been trying to explain for years.

He discovered this by looking at light. Light is just like sound. When sound is closer to us, it has a higher pitch and when it moves away, it has a lower pitch. The same is true of light. When it is close it has one color and when it moves away it has another color. This was the basis for his discovery that the universe is expanding outward in all directions. He also discovered that the farther away the objects are, the faster their expansion. This was an important discovery because of what happens in time. As time moves on there is expansion outward, but when we reverse time, there is contraction inward. Ultimately, when we reverse time, the universe constricts to a point.

Stephen Hawking. One of the most famous physicists of our time, Hawking found that with this constriction, space would get so tight that there was no more space. The curve would keep tightening. If this is true, nothing could exist in that space. How do we explain this? We currently have no way to explain it. This is a major focus of the study of physics to this day—to develop theories about the existence of the universe.

Hawking wrote that "a great many universes were created out of nothing," but "their creation does not require the intervention of some supernatural being."[14]

Although there is no physical evidence that the universe has always been here, Hawking chose to believe there is no God. His gut-level feeling that there is no creator caused him to seek some other explanation, even though there was no proof. He trusted that it was true, even though his theory provides no explanation for the creation of something from nothing apart from a creator. It's interesting that even he repeatedly used the word creation.

Charles Townes. The former chairman of the Physics Department at Columbia University, Nobel Prize winning physicist Charles Townes reportedly wrote, "In my view the question of origin seems always left unanswered if we explore for a scientific point of view alone. Thus, I believe there is a need for some religious or metaphysical explanation. I believe in the concept of God and in his existence."[15]

Charles Townes looked at the physical evidence and came to a different gut-level conclusion than Hawking—that there must be a God who exists.

Robert Jastrow. Townes's view was supported by Robert Jastrow, a Ph.D. in theoretical physics from Columbia University, an astronomer, physicist, cosmologist, and leading NASA scientist. He said, "Astronomers now find they have painted themselves into a corner because they have proven, by their own methods, that the world began abruptly in an act of creation to which you can trace the seeds of every star, every planet, every living thing in this cosmos and on the earth. And they have found that all this happened as a product of forces they cannot hope to discover....That there are what I or anyone would call supernatural forces at work is now, I think, a scientifically proven fact."[16] Jastrow looked at the evidence and came up with a gut-level conclusion that there must be a God who exists.

Albert Einstein. The issue with some researchers is their preconceived belief that there is no creator. It makes no logical sense to them. They rely on logic alone and disregard faith. They spend their time trying to develop theories to disprove the existence of God because of this.

A good example is Albert Einstein. He was a pantheist who believed there is a divine essence in all of us but that there is no creator God. His research on the Theory of Relativity led to a calculation that the universe must be expanding. He didn't like this conclusion, because it opened up the possibility that there is a supernatural being who created us.

Once again, if we reverse time, the universe comes to a specific point of creation. Because he didn't like what the evidence revealed, he introduced an equation into his formula called the "cosmological constant" that supported the belief that the universe was stagnant and not expanding.[17]

This is an example of what occurs with some scientists. They don't base their beliefs on what the evidence says, but on what they want the evidence to say. Later, Einstein would be exposed to information that he could not deny—he would meet Hubble and see the evidence that proved that his original finding was true— the universe is expanding. The evidence showed that there was a beginning point of nature and time.

I've shared what these scientists believed. What do you believe? We learn from them that it isn't a leap of faith to believe the universe is created. There is good evidence to lead us to conclude with confidence that it was created. We look at the facts and make the best conclusion from what we know to be true. It makes logical sense that someone created the universe.

The question is, "Who started it?" Who brought the first physical mass into existence? If not nature, then something supernatural that is separate from nature brought it about. This supernatural being is called God.

5

WHAT IS RIGHT AND WRONG BEHAVIOR?

Now that we know it is possible to have confidence that there is a God, what's next?

THE MORALITY QUESTION

The question is, "What is right and wrong behavior?" We want what is right and wrong to be defined. We also want to know who decides what is right and wrong. If our conclusion is there is a God who created us, we can also conclude that he determines what is right and wrong. If God created us, he made us in such a way that we can know what is right and wrong. We learned this previously. We're created in a way to feel guilt when we do wrong things and feel at peace when we do what is right. If there is no God, we define what is right and wrong.

Why is this important to us?

Right and wrong behaviors are attached to something that all of us want to experience. It's called love. Remember, we all have a desire for love. We need it. If someone loves us, they should treat us right. If someone doesn't love us, they treat us wrong. Again, our behaviors often indicate how we feel about others. They are the measurements that we use to determine if someone really cares.

Earlier, we considered reasons why more and more people are choosing not to believe in God. One connects with our desire to be accepted and not judged. I mention this again because judgment and morality are intertwined. How does it work? We decide what is right and wrong (what is moral) and we filter our behaviors according to those beliefs about right and wrong (we make judgments).

It is natural, in our desire not to be judged, that we determine morality on our terms according to how we want to behave and what we want to accomplish in life. We don't want to feel judged by others who say that what we do is wrong. The solution to this problem is to find others who agree with our way of life and to begin convincing others that our way of life is not wrong but is right.

This is why many refuse to believe in God. They want to live in a specific way, but God communicates to them that the way they choose to live is not what's best.

We can logically assume something about God. If he created us, he wants the best for what he made. He wants to protect us. He also wants us to experience what he desires for us. He wants us to live with joy. Remember, happiness is temporary and doesn't last. But joy can last forever through being in a relationship with God as his family member, a relationship no one can take away.

If his wanting to protect us and wanting us to have joy is true, then his telling us that something is not best for us is done for good reasons. He's trying to protect us from harm or to keep us from living for something that does not ultimately give us what we're looking for. With this in mind, we can think in a good way about why God would say something is wrong rather than having a bad attitude toward him because he said it's wrong.

He doesn't want what he created to be harmed. If I want to do what is right, I need to make sure that I don't harm what he has created. This would be wrong behavior. I need to ask, "Is what I'm doing harmful to others?" I can also ask, "Is what I'm doing harmful to myself?" I can know what is harmful and what is not. How?

THE DIRECTIONS

God communicates to us through the historical documents of the Bible. For example, the Ten Commandments mention some of these behaviors. We can think about commandments as the directions we need to stay on the path God wants us to travel through life.

The first four commands point out how we are to treat God and the last six how we are to treat others. Since we're still trying to decide whether to have a relationship with God, let's skip the first four. They tell us how we are to treat him as a family member. We're not to that point yet. For now, let's consider the last six, which are found in Exodus 20:12–17:

- I am to honor my father and mother. If they are parenting the right way, they are doing it to protect me and guide me on my course of life.
- I am not to murder. I would say that's harming others.I am not to commit adultery. We're to be

faithful in our commitment to the one we have married. To not be faithful is to not show love and to be harmful.

- I should not steal. To do so is harmful behavior that takes something that could be used for the survival or benefit of others.
- I am not to lie. To manipulate the truth can bring harm to others and to myself.
- I am not to covet. In other words, I am not to lust after the people or material possessions that others have. To do so is to live for something that doesn't truly satisfy my desire for joy in life and is, therefore, harmful to myself.

There are many other instructions in the Bible about right and wrong behavior. I'll give you one other example. It was written by someone that we've already learned about. It was written by Paul. He's the guy who reasoned with the Epicureans and Stoics.

Paul wrote a letter to a group of Christians who were living in a place called Galatia. They were obviously like us, struggling with doing what was right and wrong. He reminded them that we have someone within us who tells us what is right and wrong. He referred to him as God's Spirit. God speaks through him to help us know how to live to find joy. God's Spirit is that part of God that gives us our gut-level feelings.

Paul teaches them to walk by the Spirit. In doing so, he tells them to follow God's leading in how to live. Not only does he encourage them to follow God's leading, he encourages them not to live according to their own desires separate from God. He refers to living this way as living by the desires of the flesh. He teaches them that if they follow the leading of what God wants following His Spirit, there is no need to be concerned about the law (the Ten Commandments). Why? If we follow the influence of God's Spirit, we'll do what we do to protect those who God created. They'll be living the right way! Let's look at what he wrote:

> *So I say, walk by the Spirit, and you will not gratify the desires of the flesh. For the flesh desires what is contrary to the Spirit, and the Spirit what is contrary to the flesh. They are in conflict with each other, so that you are not to do whatever you want. But if you are led by the Spirit, you are not under the law. The acts of the flesh are obvious: sexual immorality, impurity and debauchery; idolatry and witchcraft; hatred, discord, jealousy, fits of rage, selfish ambition, dissensions, factions and envy; drunkenness, orgies, and the like. I warn you, as I did before, that those who live like this will not inherit the kingdom of God.*

> *But the fruit of the Spirit is love, joy, peace, forbearance, kindness, goodness, faithfulness, gentleness and self-control. Against such things there is no law. (Galatians 5:16–23)*

Why would they not inherit the kingdom of God? They wouldn't be willing to give up their way of life to follow God's way. This is the real issue for many. They don't want to give up their way of life for a life that is better. They don't know it's better. They believe their way is best. The problem is that they are trying to find happiness in temporary things. This happiness goes away, and they begin looking for something more. Remember, the Epicureans and Stoics both had this problem.

There are two lists of behaviors given in these scriptures. Let's consider them in reverse order. The second list includes our behaviors when we follow the influence of God's Spirit. They are referred to as fruits. What do we do? We love. This love gives us joy. Being in a loving relationship with the one who unconditionally loves us and showing his unconditional love to others gives us joy. When we love this way, we can be at peace with God and others.

We are to be kind to others. We are to do what is good for them, wanting the best for them. We are to be faithful and do what we say we will do, encouraging others to trust us. We are to be gentle in how we treat others, being concerned that what we say and do will be received well. We are also to practice self-control. We are not to allow others treating us in a negative way to influence how we treat them. We want to show them unconditional love and treat them in a positive way.

The first list includes those behaviors we do to please ourselves. We do what we do for our benefit and not for the benefit of those we encounter. We all have struggled with behaviors like these at points in our lives. They are also behaviors that we might not be willing to give up. It may be that one of these behaviors is keeping you from wanting to know God. It's important to know what is keeping us from wanting a relationship with him. They are called acts of the flesh—behaviors that would be considered wrong, behaviors that are not best for us. They are behaviors that hurt who God created. They can be placed in the following categories:

- Replacing God: idolatry, witchcraft
- Hurtful Attitudes: hatred, jealousy, selfishness, envy
- Causing Division or Harm: discord, dissensions, factions, rage
- Substance Abuse: drunkenness
- Sexual Behaviors: sexual immorality, impurity, debauchery, orgies

Let's consider them in more detail.

Replacing God: idolatry, witchcraft. This may not seem to be a big problem for many. After all, we don't see statues of gods around our neighborhoods that people stop by to worship. That's what I tend to think about when I hear the word idol. However, idol worship does exist in our culture today. An idol is whatever person or thing we've made our god. They (or it) is most important to us. We can recognize our god because we talk about it the most, we spend our free time with it the most, we spend our money on it the most, or we form relationships with others who share our passion for whoever or whatever it may be. It could be a celebrity, your car, your house, golfing, your job, or a litany of many other things. What or who is your god?

Hurtful Attitudes: hatred, jealousy, selfishness, envy. Life becomes a competition. We feel our value comes from being as good as or better than others, and when we don't measure up, we respond with hurtful attitudes. We hate those who are better than us. We know this because we act out to harm them. This is hateful behavior. We are jealous of those who have what we want. We act out to take it from them or keep them from having it. We are only thinking about ourselves and what we want rather than others and what they need. This selfish thought keeps us from thinking about the harm we do to those we act against. We envy others because of their success or their possession of what we desire, and we work toward sabotaging them, causing them to fail. Is your life a competition?

Causing Division or Harm: discord, dissensions, factions, rage. We begin to believe that we are always right. We push our agenda on others, not having any concern for their feelings or the reason they have different beliefs. The attitude becomes "It's me against you" or "It's us against them." This causes divisions among people. We lack regard and respect for who they are as people. We speak hurtful words, make false accusations, or act out in physical violence to force our points of view. This is seen often in the political environment, in the workplace, in neighborhood associations, in other organizational structures, and even in the family. Factions form, negative attitudes persist, and hurtful behaviors cause others to feel devalued. It hurts them. Do you push your way on others without thinking of the harm you are causing?

Substance Abuse: drunkenness. We want to feel good so we abuse substances to have a pleasurable experience. We may do this to escape some type of discomfort or to feel the physical high. Although drunkenness is mentioned, this could be the abuse of any substance used for the same purposes. We rely on these substances to deal with our pain, whatever it may be, or to make us feel good. We could make another choice. We could rely on God to help us deal with our challenges. We could also rely on our loving relationship with God to give us a spiritual high, leading us to feel true joy. Are you abusing substances to escape or to feel good?

Sexual Behaviors: sexual immorality, impurity, debauchery, orgies. Sexuality is part of the human experience. This is no surprise to God. He created us to be sexual beings for a purpose. For humanity to survive, humans need to reproduce.

> *So God created mankind in his own image, in the image of God he created them; male and female he created them. God blessed them and said to them, "Be fruitful and increase in number; fill the earth and subdue it…"*
> *(Genesis 1:27–28)*

We were told to multiply and fill the earth. He created our bodies, male and female, so we could accomplish this purpose.

Sexuality was also created to be a pleasurable experience which bound together two people who cared enough for each other to commit to one another for life. Just after God created woman, we read this in the Bible:

> *The man said, "This is now bone of my bones and flesh of my flesh; she shall be called 'woman,' for she was taken out of man." That is why a man leaves his father and mother and is united to his wife, and they become one flesh."*
> *(Genesis 2:23–24)*

The man and the woman become one flesh. They were created to connect to each other physically to become one. The body parts fit to make one flesh to reproduce and to show their love and commitment to each other. This pleasurable encounter is a gift to those who have committed themselves to one another for a lifetime.

Sexuality was never intended by God to be used as a pleasurable act to satisfy a personal desire. It was intended to be an act of service toward the one they had committed themselves to for a lifetime. We serve them by helping them feel good physically (pleasure). It's not about our pleasure, it's about our helping others experience it. However, many choose another purpose when it comes to sexuality. They engage in sexual activity aimed at their own pleasure. This is difficult to reconcile when it comes to God's view of our bodies and how he created us. This may give you more understanding about why many who believe in God value highly human life and why they view sexuality the way they do.

There has been much debate and division over the sexual behaviors of those who engage in sexual activity which is not meant for his purposes. There are those who engage in sexuality outside of a committed married relationship. There are those who have open marriages where sexuality is permitted with those other than their life partner, their spouse. There are also those who engage in sexual behaviors with the same sex.

A sexual preference that has kept many from a relationship with God is homosexuality. Knowing this is true and wanting to help as many people as possible experience a relationship with God, it is important to process why it has become a sticking point. Many involved in this lifestyle know that many Christians believe that sex is to occur between a man and a woman who are committed together in marriage. Because they disagree, it turns them off from Christianity. Why? They feel judged and not loved. Remember, we don't like feeling judged.

Please know my belief. We don't have the right to judge anyone. None do what is right at all times. We all have struggles. It is also important to me personally because three of the best friends I've had over my lifetime are gay. I want the best for them.

There is a difference between judging and giving directions about right behavior. Most people would expect others to tell people what they believe regarding the best way to live, especially if they believe it would be helpful to others. The problem is, it's easy to move from giving directions to judging others for what they do. It's not our role to judge. It's our role to point out areas that are keeping people from experiencing their best life and to help them overcome what is keeping them from experiencing it. Again, Jesus didn't judge, he pointed out selfish behavior and encouraged people to change. He was even willing to die in the place of those who were selfish so they could be forgiven and change.

Instead of judging, I want to be like Paul and empathize with those in this lifestyle by putting myself in their position. It's important to understand why people believe what they believe and understand how someone can find themselves engaged in this behavior. Empathizing is important for those on both sides of the issue. When we do this, we can have a conversation to determine what is true. It's not about judgment, it's about wanting to know what is best.

EMPATHIZING

How can I empathize? I can understand how people become involved in this lifestyle. Let me explain. All humans have attraction. We are attracted to objects, lifestyles, and people. We see something, it's attractive to us, and we want it. We see a position in society someone has, it's attractive to us, and we want it. We see someone, they are attractive to us, and we want to connect with him or her. All of us have attraction toward people. We can even have attraction for the same sex.

We learn from scientific study that physical attraction plays a role, not only in determining sexual partners, but in our forming of friendships. The National Library of Medicine determined from their study that there are five factors influencing friendships:

1. Reciprocal candor. We feel that someone understands us. There is a natural flow in our conversation with them. They make us feel comfortable.
2. Mutual interests. We have common interests. We may have the same hobby or similar ambitions.
3. Personableness. We feel that the person has a genuine interest in us. They are nice to us. They seem to care about us.
4. Similarity. We come from similar backgrounds. This may include our nationality, our race, our financial status, our graduating from the same school or other similar experiences.
5. Physical attraction. We recognize that they meet our standard of someone we consider to be attractive. He or she is someone we would want to look like. Because we know how people in a society treat attractive people, we assume he or she experiences social and professional happiness. We assume people want to be their friends and treat them differently in the workplace because of the way they look.[18]

I'll give you an example of physical attraction. I think Ryan Gosling is attractive. I don't have any desire to have sex with him, but I would love to look like him. He's fit, has hair, and I really dig the way he dresses.

I even went through a Ryan Gosling fashion phase. I would love to be his friend. There is a natural attraction that I have toward him, but this attraction only goes so far. It doesn't go beyond wanting to be his friend or to look like him.

What if I lived in a society that encouraged my attraction to grow toward the same sex? What if I lived in a culture where there was no talk about God or his plan for sexuality. What if the norm in this culture was to develop same-sex attractions and to have sexual relationships with the same sex, leading to my acceptance. Could I see myself in that society giving into the influence of the culture and becoming like others in the community? Yes, I could see where that could happen. Does that mean I'm gay? No. I don't have this desire, but I can see how it could be developed. That's the power of influence in a culture. That's also the power of wanting acceptance. What I've described is the culture that many live within. Because of this, I see why the number of those involved in this lifestyle continues to grow.

As I mentioned, it is important to understand both perspectives. Christians can empathize with people who are gay, but it is also important for those who are a part of this lifestyle to know why some Christians believe what they believe. Some who are gay believe that Christians only want to condemn others. The truth is, many Christians (like me) don't want to judge or condemn, they are acting out of love for the other person and wanting them to experience their best life.

If you are a part of this lifestyle, I want to help you empathize. Have you ever thought about why the gay lifestyle would not be God's plan? Let's consider this. To help us, we'll do something. Imagine there is no God. What if it were just us, human beings, needing to continue on. A logical conclusion to ensure humanity's existence would be to produce more humans. Doing so could be seen as a service to humanity. We're doing something for the survival of our species. This can be seen in history as marriages were arranged and children were expected to be born so that families could continue to live on their land, produce their crops and succeed in their businesses.

Having children was seen as a blessing to the family and as a service to the community. They showed love, proving that they cared for those in their family. It also gave them a sense of purpose. They were to help each other survive and succeed. To choose not to do this and deliberately refuse to marry and have children was looked down upon. They would not be fulfilling their needed roles to continue as a people. Because of this, they believed doing so was wrong. They came to this conclusion without God saying anything.

Now let's put God back in the picture. If there is a God who made us in a way to multiply and continue and created sexuality as a gift to those who committed themselves to each other for a lifetime, don't you think that he may have an issue with those who choose to change it? As we've already learned, God's purpose for sexuality is service to others. It's to serve the community by reproducing, ensuring our survival and success, and to serve our partner by helping him or her feel the pleasure that comes from sex occurring in a committed marriage. It's not about our serving ourselves.

God knows that self-serving sex is not what is best for us. We experience what is best when we do what we do for the good of others. Our showing love to them in this way gives us the joy we desire. Our living for happiness from a pleasurable experience doesn't provide for us what we need.

I get that this is difficult. There are issues that cause us to lean in this direction. Let's think about these. We've learned about attraction, but we need to consider it in more detail by responding to what many people say. If you struggle with homosexuality, you may be saying, "But Tim, you don't understand. I was born this way!" Once again, I can relate, but in a different way.

Science reveals the role that hormones like estrogen and testosterone play in our sexuality. Some believe that when these hormones don't match our physical makeup of being a man or woman, that it can lead to our attraction for the same sex. I understand how this could occur. Although some don't agree with this, I can see how this could happen.

I was also born with a physical condition, but in a different way. I don't have a hormone imbalance, I have a chemical imbalance. I have an improper amount of serotonin. Because of this, I am bipolar and suffer from Obsessive Compulsive Disorder (OCD). I've been diagnosed and treated for both. Before I go on, please don't assume something as I write this. I'm NOT saying that people who are gay have a mental illness. I'm pointing out the difference that the chemicals in our bodies can make. If my serotonin imbalance, which I was born with, can lead me to have these conditions, then it makes sense that the same could be true for those who have a hormone imbalance leading to attraction for the same sex.

You might be asking, "If this is true, does this make the behavior acceptable?" To answer that, I'll tell you more about my issue. There are two types of behaviors that are common with people with my bipolar diagnosis. It's called bipolar type II or hypomania. The first is promiscuous sexual behavior. The other is risky financial behavior in making purchases of products you cannot afford. My struggle is with the second of these. I've purchased eight boats. There were times I had more than one at a time.

Don't judge me! Remember, humans don't like this. This behavior has put my family in financial jeopardy in the past.

Imagine, however, that I struggle with the first behavior. Let's say I'm married and I begin to have multiple relationships with other women outside of my marriage because of my bipolar tendencies. Is it okay for me to cheat on my wife? Can I say, "It's okay for me to behave this way. I'm bipolar!?" I know my wife wouldn't accept that explanation. I'm in a relationship with her and need to be true to my commitment to my wife. My sexual relationship is reserved for her and her alone.

What do I do if I have this struggle? I find help! I secure the assistance of someone who can help me overcome these desires so I remain faithful. My gut says this is the right way to behave. Just because we were born a certain way, doesn't give us a free pass to behave in an unhealthy manner.

Attraction is not the only factor that influences people to be engaged in the gay lifestyle. There are others. You may also say, "But Tim, you don't understand. I was sexually abused." You may have been molested by someone of the same sex, causing you to have these attractions. You may have been abused by someone of the opposite sex and now are repulsed by the idea of having this type of sex again because of it. Each of these examples affects us. They cause trauma. How do we deal with this? We seek help to work through this trauma so that it can be overcome.

What do we learn from all of this? We decide on our own what we believe about this lifestyle. Some continue to believe that it is the best way for them to live. They can empathize with what some Christians believe, but they don't agree. If this is true of you, know that your disagreement with those who are Christians doesn't cause them to stop caring about you. They still love you and want the best for you. Their fear is that you're missing it.

But what if your empathizing with Christians has caused you to think in a new way and changed your perspective? What if you now believe that there is a better life for you following God's plan for sexuality? What do you do?

Change comes through the influence of our minds and hearts. When we change the mind, we can have a change of heart. It is possible to change. If you are involved in this lifestyle, you may be saying, "But Tim, I just don't see how I could change and have a relationship with the opposite sex. How could this happen?" I'm not saying that your attractions will change, but I am saying that it is possible.

Attractions can change. We've already learned that we know what it's like to have attraction for both sexes and how these attractions can be encouraged to develop. If I can understand how I, who does not have homosexual attractions, could develop those attractions, then I can also understand how someone who has homosexual attractions could develop attractions for the opposite sex. Remember, attraction can be involved in friendship. This helps us understand how we can change. We begin friendships with the opposite sex. These friendships often cause our attraction to grow.

There are many examples of people who began friendships with someone of the opposite sex without any attraction. The more they learned about each other, the stronger their bond became and the more their attraction grew. It led to a committed relationship. People from the outside look at the couple and say, "I don't get why they are attracted to each other. They don't seem to fit!" It may be that they don't both meet our criteria for being attractive. Attraction is not only about looks, it's also about our personalities and our character. It can grow, causing our heart to become passionate toward the other, leading us into a committed lasting relationship.

A WILLINGNESS TO CHANGE

Now that we have looked at each category in more detail, let's consider our own behaviors. Do you struggle with any of these? Do you feel like they are wrong or right? Are they truly fulfilling you? If you believe they are, you may see no need to change. If they don't, you may be willing.

I know I have written much about sexuality, but Jesus taught about another struggle more often—our attraction to money. He met a young guy who had this issue. We read:

> *Just then a man came up to Jesus and asked, "Teacher, what good thing must I do to get eternal life?" "Why do you ask me about what is good?" Jesus replied. "There is only One who is good. If you want to enter life, keep the commandments." "Which ones?" he inquired. Jesus replied, "'You shall not murder, you shall not commit adultery, you shall not steal, you shall not give false testimony, honor your father and mother,' and 'love your neighbor as yourself.'" "All these I have kept," the young man said. "What do I still lack?" Jesus answered, "If you want to be perfect, go, sell your possessions and give to the poor, and you will have treasure in heaven. Then come, follow me." When the young man heard this, he went away sad, because he had great wealth. Then Jesus said to his disciples, "Truly I tell you, it is hard for someone who is rich to enter the kingdom of heaven." (Matthew 19:16–23)*

After hearing that he would be required to give away his wealth, he walked away. Why? His money was more important to him than having a relationship with God. It was more important than helping those God had created. It kept him from having a relationship with God, a relationship that would allow him to have eternal life. It was his idol.

What would cause us to be willing to give up our idol, whatever it is? If it no longer fulfills us and we're wanting something more. Would you be willing to give up what you're living for to experience a better life?

6

WHAT HAPPENS WHEN WE DO WHAT IS WRONG?

Knowing right and wrong is taught in most of the world's major religions. There is another common theme. We need help connecting with God. We need someone or something to tell us how we experience him. We need a go-between who tells us the rules (or the laws) we are to follow. We can illustrate it like this:

GOD

↑

Law

↑

Religion

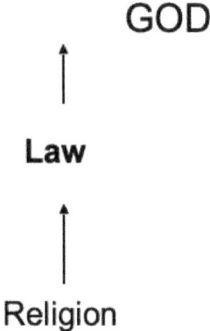

Those who give us these rules are known as mediators. They are go-betweens. They tell us what we need to do to form a relationship with someone else. Karen Henly also does a great job in describing them. Let's take a look at some of these mediators.[19]

JUDAISM

In Judaism, the law of God was revealed to Moses and recorded in the first five books of the Hebrew scriptures known as the Torah. The Ten Commandments are found in this portion of scripture. The Torah is the go-between.

BUDDHISM

Buddhists have the dharma, which means cosmic law and order, but is also applied to the teachings of the Buddha. The Five Precepts are an example of the rules to be followed in Buddhism. They are a code of conduct to help people behave in a moral and ethical way. They include refraining from taking a person's life, taking what is not given to us, doing wrong in sexual behaviors, using our words in the wrong ways by lying and speaking harshly, and using intoxicants that cloud our minds.[20] Dharma is the go-between.

ISLAM

The Qur'an is believed to have been given to Muhammad and contains the laws that are to be followed to know their God. These laws dictate how they are to live. The website Why Islam (whyislam.org) explains the moral expectations of humanity in relation to God and to each other. The site reveals this by beginning with statements from the Qur'an.

It is not righteousness that ye turn your faces toward East or West; but it is righteousness to believe in Allah and the Last Day, and the Angels, and the Book, and the Messengers; to spend of your substance, out of love for Him, for your kin, for orphans, for the needy, for the wayfarer, for those who ask, and for the ransom of slaves; to be steadfast in prayer and practice regular charity; to fulfil the contracts which ye have made; and to be firm and patient, in pain (or suffering) and adversity, and throughout all periods of panic. Such are the people of truth, the Allah-fearing." (Al-Qur'an 2:177)[21]

The Qur'an is the go-between.

GREEK RELIGIONS

For the Greeks, the logos is a spiritual force that speaks the word of truth and reason. It's defined as "the divine reason implicit in the cosmos, ordering it and giving it form and meaning."[22] It is a mysterious essence that guides them to knowledge, a knowledge of how to live. The logos is the go-between.

What do we learn from all of this? There is a prevailing common belief. The mediator tells those who believe in them the rules that must be followed so that they can experience their God. They tell them how to live. These behaviors are defined and become laws. They believe that they must be followed to work their way into connecting with their God.

What happens if we don't obey the law? We are separated from God. We can illustrate it like this:

GOD

Law

↑

Religion

What causes the separation? It's called sin. This is a common word understood by other religions. We can illustrate it like this:

GOD

sin

Law

↑

Religion

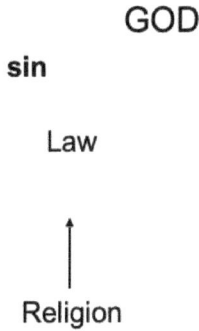

The word sin is an old military term which means to miss the mark. A commander would take a soldier out to shoot a target. If the soldier missed the target he would say, "Soldier, you sinned."

Paul taught this to the Christians in Rome. He wrote, *"...for all have sinned and fall short of the glory of God..." (Romans 3:23)*

To bring glory to God is to reveal what he is about. He is a God of love. We sin when we miss the mark of showing God's love. When we show God's love, we put others before ourselves, leading us to live a moral life.

We treat others the way we want to be treated. We want to be loved. This is a good description of right and wrong behavior. We know this is true in our gut. We feel it on a spiritual level. We feel this is true without having to be taught that it is true. We want to be treated in a way that protects us, provides for our needs, and helps us to grow to reach our potential. That's showing God's love.

The Bible tells us who God is. We read this in 1 John 4:8 which says, "Whoever does not love does not know God, because God is love."

Again, to bring glory to God, we love like he loves. We also read in 1 John these words: *"Dear friends, since God so loved us, we also ought to love one another. No one has ever seen God; but if we love one another, God lives in us and his love is made complete in us." (1 John 4:11–12)*

God's love is shown when we do what is best for others and when we do what is best for ourselves to protect who God created us to be. To harm others or ourselves is to fall short of showing God's love. That's the problem. We have all sinned and caused harm. Our sinning keeps us from being in a relationship with God. God can't be in a relationship with someone who chooses to be selfish. This is logical. Relationships can't survive when there is selfishness. Our sin keeps us from connecting with him.

Now we can begin to understand the difference between Christianity and other religions. Other religions believe that we can earn a relationship with God, while Christians believe that we cannot earn our way to God. We know that we don't always do what is right. Knowing that we can't earn a relationship with him, we rely on God to bridge the gap. We don't work our way to God, he comes to us. How? Through love! We can illustrate it like this:

```
              GOD
  sin           |
                |
                ↓
  Law         Love


        ↑
        |
        |
     Religion
```

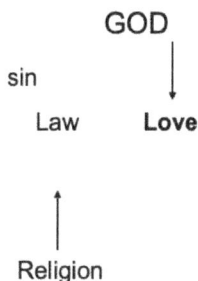

How do we know he loves us? We need someone to show us and tell us. The Bible teaches: *"For God so loved the world that he gave his one and only Son, that whoever believes in him shall not perish but have eternal life." (John 3:16)* God sent Jesus to show His love to us. We don't need someone to come and tell us the laws that we are to follow, we need someone to come and tell us that we are loved by God even though we break the law.

God loves the imperfect. We need someone to tell us that God wants to forgive us and has given us a way to be forgiven for our imperfections. We need someone to tell us that God still wants to have a relationship with us even though we've been imperfect. We need someone to tell us the truth—the gospel truth!

We need a new kind of mediator, not just a mediator who tells us the rules, but a mediator who tells us how we can be made right when we break them. The question is, "How can we have a relationship with God if we have sinned?"

God did send His son Jesus to us to show His love to us, but the truth is, we don't deserve this. We deserve to be punished for the things that we do wrong. We can illustrate it like this...

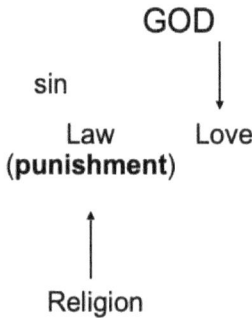

$$
\begin{array}{c}
\textbf{GOD} \\
\big\downarrow \\
\text{sin} \qquad \qquad \\
\text{Law} \qquad \text{Love} \\
\textbf{(punishment)} \\
\big\uparrow \\
\text{Religion}
\end{array}
$$

The spiritual crime is our breaking the law, and the punishment for that crime is death. We connect our breaking the law with the punishment of death. We can illustrate it like this:

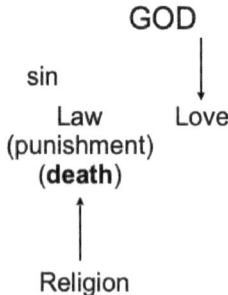

$$
\begin{array}{c}
\textbf{GOD} \\
\big\downarrow \\
\text{sin} \qquad \qquad \\
\text{Law} \qquad \text{Love} \\
\text{(punishment)} \\
\textbf{(death)} \\
\big\uparrow \\
\text{Religion}
\end{array}
$$

Why death? When our selfish desires grow, it leads us to sin, to do what is wrong. We are selfish and do unloving things. We sin by hurting others and hurting ourselves. Sin, at its deepest stage, leads to death. It's the most harmful thing we can do. We take someone's life. It's the worst way we can hurt others. This is also taught in our historical document, the Bible: "Then, after desire has conceived, it gives birth to sin; and sin, when it is full-grown, gives birth to death." (James 1:15) We're punished for the worst of what we could do. Death is our punishment.

This punishment comes in two ways. There is a physical death and a spiritual death. We know that we will all die one day. Physical death came into the world when mankind sinned against God in the beginning of creation. Adam and Eve disobeyed God and their eventual death would be the consequence. This continues on today for us. There is another death. It is a spiritual death.

After our physical death, our spirit continues on. The spirit of those who do not have a relationship with God cannot be where He is. They will be separated from Him forever. God lives in Heaven which means that those who do not have a relationship with Him will be separated from Him in another location. The Bible calls it Hell. Jesus taught about both Heaven and Hell. He gave a description of Heaven to a thief who was being crucified next to him. This man stood up for Jesus and he told him *"Truly I tell you, today you will be with me in paradise." (Luke 23:43)* He described it as paradise. It is a place where there is no more pain, suffering or selfishness. Jesus also described Hell. He was teaching about those who do not treat others in the right way and made a statement. He said, *""Then they will go away to eternal punishment,..." (Matthew 25:46)* It's a place where we will be punished for our selfishness along with all others who refused to admit their failures to God.

God doesn't want this for any person! That is why He took action. He sent to us a Savior. We can illustrate it like this:

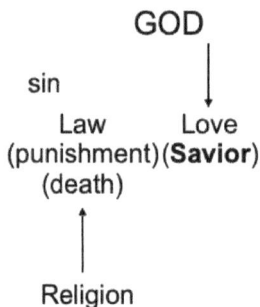

GOD

sin

Law   Love
(punishment)(**Savior**)
(death)

Religion

What is the solution for this problem? We need someone to take our punishment. A savior is one who takes our place. It would be like one of my sisters choosing to take the punishment for something that I did wrong in my family so I wouldn't have to. By the way, this never happened! Why would someone do this? Only because they love us.

Remember, God loves us even though we break the

law and deserve punishment. He proves this love by sending someone who loves like he does to show that love to us through sacrifice, the greatest form of love. We need someone willing to give their life for us. This happened through the person of Jesus. We can illustrate it like this:

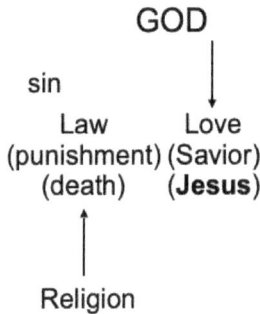

GOD

sin

Law   Love
(punishment) (Savior)
(death)   (**Jesus**)

Religion

The Bible teaches: *"But God demonstrates his own love for us in this: While we were still sinners, Christ died for us." (Romans 5:8)* We also read: *"This is how God showed his love among us: He sent his one and only Son into the world that we might live through him. 10 This is love: not that we loved God, but that he loved us and sent his Son as an atoning sacrifice for our sins." (1 John 4:9-10)* Jesus died for our sins on the cross so that we wouldn't need to die ourselves. He died so we could live!

Not only did he die for us, God also resurrected Jesus by bringing him back to life three days later. There was a reason for his resurrection. He proved his power over the worst of what Satan could do to us and provided a way for us to come back to life in Heaven after our death. Because Jesus came back to life, so can we!

God did all of this so we could have a relationship with Him. We can illustrate it like this:

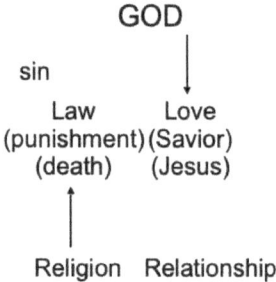

```
              GOD
                │
    sin         │
                ▼
    Law        Love
(punishment)(Savior)
  (death)    (Jesus)
     ▲
     │
     │
 Religion  Relationship
```

To have this relationship, we must be forgiven. We can illustrate it like this:

```
              GOD
                │
    sin         │
                ▼
    Law        Love
(punishment)(Savior)
  (death)    (Jesus)
     ▲         forgiveness
     │
 Religion  Relationship
```

We are forgiven when the punishment for our sins is paid for and we accept what has been done for us. We can illustrate it like this...

GOD

sin

Law   Love
(punishment) (Savior)
(death)   (Jesus)

                forgiveness
                (accept)

Religion   Relationship

When we accept the forgiveness that is offered, the gap between us and God has been bridged and we have a relationship with Him. The question is, how do we accept what Jesus did for us?

We accept this forgiveness by believing in what Jesus did for us and committing to follow him. The Bible teaches us... *If you declare with your mouth, "Jesus is Lord," and believe in your heart that God raised him from the dead, you will be saved. 10 For it is with your heart that you believe and are justified, and it is with your mouth that you profess your faith and are saved. (Romans 10:9-10)* We do this through prayer. The Bible also teaches... for, *"Everyone who calls on the name of the Lord will be saved."(Romans 10:13)* We pray the ABC's! We ADMIT, BELIEVE and COMMIT. We pray a prayer like this....

PRAYER OF ACCEPTANCE

Dear God, I ADMIT that I have sinned and ask for your forgiveness. I BELIEVE that Jesus died on the cross to take the punishment for my sins and was resurrected to provide a way for me to live forever with you in Heaven. I COMMIT to follow Jesus as the Lord of my life as I live to become like him. I pray this in Jesus' name. Amen.

How can this prayer make the difference? It's like a wedding ceremony. Before the woman and man make their vows of commitment they are a bride and a groom. After they make their vows of commitment they are family. They are a husband and a wife. That is the power of our accepting what Jesus did for us and our committing to follow him. This commitment makes us family!

We know that Jesus died on the cross. Historical books other than the Bible tell us about Jesus and his crucifixion. That is why other religions don't deny him. We know he died on the cross. It becomes personal when I know he died on the cross to forgive me of my sins and when I accept what he did. It's an action gift that we receive. We read in the Bible – *"Yet to all who did receive him, to those who believed in his name, he gave the right to become children of God..." (John 1:12)*

My hope is that you will receive the gift of God's forgiveness through what Jesus did for you through his death and resurrection. I encourage you to pray the prayer from above and become a part of God's family right now.

If you made the decision to accept the forgiveness God has offered you through Jesus, you may be asking – "What do I do now?" It's time to let people know about your new identity. You are a child of God. You are a part of God's family. One way we do this is through doing what Jesus commanded us to do. He said, *"Therefore go and make disciples of all nations, baptizing them in the name of the Father and of the Son and of the Holy Spirit... (Matthew 28:19)*

Being baptized communicates your belief in the death, burial and resurrection of Jesus. Remember, these are the three beliefs that all Christians have in common. You're letting people know that you trust that Jesus did this for you. Baptism is a visual picture of these beliefs. When you stand in the water it symbolizes that you believe Jesus died on the cross. When you are put under the water, it symbolizes your belief that Jesus was buried. When you come out from under the water, it symbolized that you believe that Jesus was resurrected. You want people to know that Jesus did this for you, but you also want people who see your baptism to know that they can have the same joy that you're experiencing through Jesus. If you have accepted what Jesus has done for you, you can have joy knowing that no one can take your relationship with God away from you.

WHY JESUS IS THE ONLY WAY TO A RELATIONSHIP WITH GOD

Did you pray to accept God's forgiveness and become a part of his family or are you continuing to consider what to do? You may be asking, "Why is Jesus the only way to God?" After all, one of the main criticisms of Christianity is that Christians are narrow-minded believing that Jesus is the only way to having a relationship with God. Why can't there be another way to Him? Let's think about why Jesus is the way to God. He's the way because he meets the requirements of being a love mediator. What are the requirements?

THE LOVE MEDIATOR

We need someone who is both human and God. We need someone who connects the physical and spiritual worlds. Because we need to be connected to God, we need someone who is both God and human. It's like someone who is mixed race. They have two parents. One is of one race and the other is of a different background. The child knows what it is to be both. This describes

Jesus well. We need someone who has a Father who is supernatural and has power over all nature and a mother who is natural, connecting him to humanity. His Father was supernatural and his mother was natural. Because he had a natural mother, he knew what it was like to feel pain and death. He had emotions. Because he had a supernatural Father, he knew what it was like to have power over natural things.We need someone who is over nature. He proved this connection through the miracles he performed, healing those who were sick and bringing people back to life. Only the One who knows what it's like to be both is capable of bringing both together.

We need someone who is sinless. We need someone who doesn't miss the mark. We need one who is always moral and does what is right. If he were a failure like us, we wouldn't respect him. Why would we listen to him?

We need someone who has the right desire. We need someone who wants us to be forgiven and not be punished. He doesn't hold a grudge against us and want us to be judged even though we deserve it. He doesn't want us to suffer the consequence for our failures.

We need someone who is willing to make the ultimate sacrifice. We need someone who is willing to do whatever is necessary to allow us to be forgiven and have a relationship with God. We need someone who is willing to die for us.

We need someone to come back to life. We need someone who cannot be stopped by death. If we want to come back to life after our death and live with God in heaven, we need to trust in someone who literally came back to life after he was dead. It's the greatest example of his supernatural power over nature. If he has the power to come back to life, he has the power to bring us back to life. This gives us hope. We know that we will one day die, but God has the power to bring us back to life through the Savior Jesus. We die to one world and come to life in another. We go from Mom's home to Dad's home.

There is only one who meets the criteria of a Savior—Jesus. That is why Jesus said about himself, "I am the way and the truth and the life. No one comes to the Father except through me" (John 14:6). When we understand what is needed to have a relationship with God, we understand that to believe in Jesus is not narrow-minded, it gives us hope of reconciling with God.

I know what you might be thinking. Did he really come back to life? Believing that someone can come back to life for many is a big stretch. Why would we believe this happened? This moves us into the next fundamental question.

7

IS THERE LIFE AFTER DEATH?

Not only do we desire love, we also desire eternity. We have a longing for something beyond this life. We don't want this to be the end of us. It's the reason why we've all wondered if there is something more.

THE DESTINY QUESTION

Not only do we want to know if there is life after death, we want to know what it's like and how we can experience it. We've just learned how we can. Those who accept what Jesus did for them by taking their punishment for their sins and believing in his resurrection will live forever.

Do you believe this? Do you believe everything needed to make this decision? You might have a hang-up like that of many others. Did Jesus really come back to life?

This is an important question, because it is the one factor that makes Christianity different from all other religions. They are based on people who lived, died, and are buried. Christianity is the only religion based on someone who lived, died, was buried, and then came back to life.

Do you believe in the resurrection? Can you come to a logical conclusion that it happened? Let me see if I can help you try.

Lee Strobel, in his book *The Case for Christ*, gives a great understanding of what people believe about the resurrection on both sides of the issue. He pointed out that there were many who tried to disprove this event, and he shared their claims.[23]

FOUR CLAIMS FROM RESURRECTION SKEPTICS

There are four claims made by those who are skeptical about the resurrection:

He was resuscitated, not resurrected. Some didn't believe he was really dead. They believed he was in a deep sleep state that happened from a slow heart rate. They believe that being placed in a cold tomb woke him up and allowed him to escape. This theory is called the swoon theory. The problem with this theory is the illogical assumption that Jesus could have survived what happened to him. He was flogged, beaten, and then nailed in both his hands and feet to the cross. If that weren't enough, a soldier stabbed him in the side to make sure he was dead.

He was buried or eaten by animals. The typical procedure for a crucified criminal was to leave his body on the cross to be eaten by animals or to be thrown into a common grave for the same purpose. This doesn't gel with the what the historical accounts of the crucifixion tell us. His body was taken by Joseph of Arimathea, a member of the Sanhedrin council that convicted Jesus, to be placed in a tomb.

His body was stolen by his disciples. Some believe it was a part of a big conspiracy. They believe the disciples stole his body to make it appear that he was resurrected. There is a problem with this belief as well. Their idea of who the Messiah would be had been crushed. They believed that anyone crucified was cursed by God. They also believed that the Messiah wouldn't die. That's why they bugged out after he died and went in different directions.

There are inconsistencies in the story of the resurrection, therefore it is not true. Some of the accounts in the historical documents are not consistent. This is true. However, the details that aren't consistent are secondary elements of the historical account. The main events of the crucifixion are the same. They include Joseph of Arimathea taking the body of Jesus and putting it in a tomb, a small group of women who were followers of Jesus visiting the tomb on the Sunday morning after his crucifixion and discovering that Jesus was gone, and then a vision of angels saying that Jesus is risen. Because these events are consistent, it has historical validity. What about the evidence that he did come back to life?

FIVE EVIDENCES OF RESURRECTION REALITY

The disciples died for their beliefs. At first, the disciples scattered but then came back together. They quit their jobs and started sharing with others the same message—Jesus is alive! Why? They claimed they had seen him. Paul records for us those who had seen him.

For what I received I passed on to you as of first importance: that Christ died for our sins according to the Scriptures, that he was buried, that he was raised on the third day according to the Scriptures, and that he appeared to Cephas, and then to the Twelve. After that, he appeared to more than five hundred of the brothers and sisters at the same time, most of whom are still living, though some have fallen asleep. Then he appeared to James, then to all the apostles, and last of all he appeared to me also, as to one abnormally born. (1 Corinthians 15:3–8)

No one could convince them to deny what they had seen. They believed it so much they were willing to be tortured for their beliefs. Most of them were executed in awful ways because of their belief in Jesus's resurrection. Why would they do this for a lie? Their willingness to die for it is evidence of its truth.

The conversion of skeptics. Some who didn't believe in Jesus before the resurrection came to believe in him after seeing the risen Jesus. There are two powerful examples.

First is James, the brother of Jesus. He and Jesus's other family members were embarrassed about Jesus while he alive (John 7:5). As we just read in 1 Corinthians 15, Jesus appeared to James after his resurrection. This changed James. Another historical book, Antiquities, by the historian Flavius Josephus, tells us that James became the leader of the Christian church in Jerusalem. He was stoned to death because of his belief in Jesus.

Second is Paul, whom Jesus appeared to (when he was still known as Saul) on the road to Damascus in the form of a bright light that blinded him. Jesus asked

Paul why he was persecuting him. Paul was healed of his blindness and then dedicated his life to sharing the message about Jesus to the Gentiles (non-Jews). Before this time, he was having Christians killed to stop Jesus's movement.

Changes to key social structures. Jewish people follow strict social structures. It's a part of what makes Jewish people Jews. After Jesus's resurrection, his disciples (who were Jews) stopped practicing some of these social practices. They no longer believed they needed to offer an animal sacrifice for the forgiveness of their sins. They now believed that Jesus was the final sacrifice. They no longer believed that you were connected to God through obeying the commandments. We are incapable of following the law always and therefore can't earn a relationship with God. They no longer worshipped on the Sabbath but began worshipping on Sunday, acknowledging the day of the week that Jesus rose from the dead. They no longer believed that God was one person but expressed who he is in three persons—the Father, Son, and Holy Spirit. They understood Jesus to be the same as God (John 14:9). Jews believed that a man could not be God. Jesus's followers no longer believed that the Messiah was going to be a political leader who would destroy the Roman empire. They now believed that he would save the world from sin through his death and resurrection. By abandoning these practices, they were risking their souls being damned to hell. Why would they do this if the resurrection were not true?

Communion and baptism. They also created some new social structures. They began to meet in their homes and have a meal together to remember and symbolize their belief in the death of Jesus on the cross. They broke bread to remember that his body had been broken by the torturous acts of the soldiers and drank to remind them of the blood that Jesus shed on the cross for the forgiveness of our sins. They also adapted another tradition—baptism. The Jewish people were familiar with baptism. They baptized Gentiles who were converting to Judaism. It was called proselyte baptism. They would do this in the authority of the God of Israel. Christians baptized in a new way, symbolizing their belief in the death, burial, and resurrection of Jesus and did so in the name of the Father, Son, and the Spirit, once again placing Jesus on the same level as God the Father, which was against Jewish belief.

The belief of the church. Soon after the resurrection, the people began to gather together and all followed the same belief. This is also found in 1 Corinthians 15. Paul wrote to the church at Corinth, *"For what I received I passed on to you as of first importance: that Christ died for our sins according to the Scriptures, that he was buried, that he was raised on the third day according to the Scriptures…" (1 Corinthians 15:3–4).*

There is a creed that has remained common in all Christian churches since this time: We believe Christ died for our sins. We believe he was buried. We believed that he was raised again on the third day. The church continued to spread and has become what it is today as we continue to share these beliefs as Christians.

What do we learn from all of this?

Many logical thinkers have come to the conclusion that Jesus did come back to life and that he is the one that we need. It is my hope that you have come to reason and believe that Jesus is the way to have a relationship with God. If you did not pray to accept what Jesus did for your forgiveness earlier, I encourage you to make that decision now. Let me ask you some questions:

- **Do you believe God exists?** After looking at the evidence, do you believe that God created the universe and that we are not an accident? Do you believe He is separate from nature and has power over all things?
- **Do you believe you have missed the mark and have sinned?** Do you know deep down what is right and wrong and that you don't measure up to who you were created to be? Do you know you don't always do what is good and loving?

- **Do you believe that God still loves you and wants to have a relationship with you?** Do you believe that God sending Jesus to show His love for you is proof that He wants you?
- **Do you believe that Jesus is the way to have a relationship with God?** Do you believe that he came to earth to show you how to live, took the punishment for your sin and was resurrected to allow you to also live forever with God in heaven?

If you believe these things, you believe what is necessary to accept the forgiveness that God offers you. A relationship with God can begin right now through accepting the gift of forgiveness that He is offering you through prayer. Do you remember the prayer? Here it is again…

PRAYER OF ACCEPTANCE

Dear God, I ADMIT that I have sinned and ask for your forgiveness. I BELIEVE that Jesus died on the cross to take the punishment for my sins and was resurrected to provide a way for me to live forever with you in Heaven. I COMMIT to follow Jesus as the Lord of my life as I live to become like him. I pray this in Jesus' name. Amen.

If you have accepted what Jesus has done for you, you can have joy knowing that no one can take your relationship with God away from you. The Bible teaches:

> *For I am convinced that neither death nor life, neither angels nor demons, neither the present nor the future, nor any powers, neither height nor depth, nor anything else in all creation, will be able to separate us from the love of God that is in Christ Jesus our Lord. (Romans 8:38–39)*

ARE YOU ON THE FENCE?

If you are continuing to consider accepting forgiveness but have not made the decision to do so, what is holding you back? Here's the deal. I'm not going to assume that you have accepted what Jesus has done for you, even though I've shared with you how we become part of God's family. If you have, that's awesome! If you haven't, I get that you may not be ready. You may not yet believe that accepting Jesus is what you need. You're placing your hope in there being another way.

This is a conversation, and I anticipated that you might feel this way. I want to share with you information about something we all need that may help you as you make your decision.

8

WHAT DO I NEED?

We all have the same need. We need hope! Do you have it?

Those who have hope without God, may not see a need for him. Those who do not have hope may be open to the possibility that it can be achieved through knowing him.

Science reveals to us our need for hope. This really smart guy named Adam P. Stern, a medical doctor and assistant professor of psychiatry at Harvard Medical School, shares the important aspects of hope. He wrote that it is an essential component of our well-being and that through hope we find ways to oppose the dread of life's dangers.

Stern described hope as an aspirational feeling that circumstances can improve and that we can persist. It's important because it affects how we feel about ourselves. He points out that hope protects against depression and suicide. It plays a role in human existence from a young age, affecting our health, quality of life, self-esteem, and our sense of purpose. Hope also develops our maturity and resilience and has the power to get us through difficulties as we process events that seem insurmountable.[24]

We do all need hope. If we feel hopeless, we're looking to find the hope that can sustain us. The question is, "What do we place our hope in?"

A definition is needed for us to better understand hope. A quick search on Dictionary.com reveals to us that it is "the feeling that what is wanted can be had or that events will turn out for the best."[25] From this definition, we can ask ourselves two questions:

What do I want in the future? What type of future world do you want to live in?

How do I want things to turn out in the future? What good do I want to see from what I'm going through?

What do we learn from this? Hope is about the future. It is also a feeling. Putting these together, we understand that hope is a feeling that we have about the future.

Because hope is a feeling, it can be associated with

our emotional state. This once again reveals to us its importance. Psychologists study hope as a means to help people deal with their emotional struggles. They believe that if hope can be developed, optimism about the future can replace the hopelessness people feel about life, which leads to unhealthy emotional states. We need to believe that things can be better in the future. The question is how?

Those who have studied hope believe it comes from the actions we perform that lead us to have the future that we desire. This helps answer the question "How do you want things to turn out in the future?" I have hope when I believe that I can change it.

The study of hope began with the work of psychologist C. Rick Snyder, Ph.D., who set in motion much of the research that is currently being performed today. He defined hope as "the perceived capability to derive pathways to desired goals, and motivate oneself via agency thinking to use those pathways."[26]

What does that mean? We could state it in this way: We have hope when we have a vision for our future (goals we want to achieve), develop a pathway of actions to accomplish that vision, and are motivated to do it. This motivation is influenced by belief. Hope requires belief. We must believe that this future is possible.

According to this scientific information, we become more hopeful when we believe we have a bearing on what happens in the future. We set goals that we can accomplish which will lead to the result we desire. The question now is, "Am I capable to achieve the desired result alone?"

Much of what we've learned centers on what we can do to accomplish the goals we set for ourselves. What if we are faced with a situation that is leading to a future that we have no ability to change on our own? If we rely on ourselves only, we lose hope. If I am limited in my abilities to change the future, to maintain hope I must partner with someone who is capable of doing what I am incapable of doing.

If I am sick, and I am not a doctor, I can enlist the help of a physician to help me overcome my sickness. But what if I'm sick and I'm not a doctor and the physician that I partner with can't do anything to cure me of my illness? What then? Do I lose hope? If there is no other source which has more capabilities, then the answer to that question is yes. I lose hope.

How could I regain hope? Is there someone else who can help me overcome my challenge? If there is no one, I have no hope for being well in my future. If there is someone, I can have hope.

Those who believe in God believe there is someone more capable than a doctor with limited ability to heal us. We believe that a supernatural God can. He has power over all physical things. Therefore, we have hope.

Let's think about Paul again. He was blinded on the

road to Damascus. He had no hope of his own capabilities making the situation better. He needed someone who had the power to do what no human being could do. He needed what Jesus could do with his supernatural power.

In moments of hopelessness, people search for God. The hopeless event is a wake-up call that we aren't powerful enough for every situation. We need someone more powerful than us. I've used the illustration of being physically unwell, but it can apply to any situation where we need the help of someone who can do more than what a human can do. We need someone who has supernatural power.

We learned about God's ability to bring nature into existence. If he can bring it into existence, he can also control it. He is the one capable to help me with struggles humanity can't fix. Because of this, I have hope that he can do something in my future to make my future better.

What if this supernatural power doesn't heal me or solve my problem? Can I still have hope?

Hope comes in other ways. Wouldn't it be great to be in a world where there were no problems? Wouldn't it be amazing to be in a place where there were no sickness, death, bills, or bullies? This gets us back to the question "What do you want in the future?" We want to live in a place like the one just described. We maintain hope when we believe in a future world without pain and suffering. Sounds like heaven to me!

What would make it better? To be there with the one

we love! There may be a person in your life that you deeply love. If you're having difficulties and you've been away from them during this time, knowing that you will see them in the future gives you hope. The relationship is important—it might be what is most important to you. Our longing to be with someone whom we love and whom we know also loves us gives us hope. We're looking toward a future when we are with God, the one who loves us unconditionally, in a place where there are no problems.

We're longing for a time when we are at peace with the one we care for the most. This gives us hope. We know this world is not all there is. It's broken. There is a home in heaven to look to if we are part of God's family. We maintain our hope knowing we are going to be with the one we love in his home.

Seeing Christians who are at the end of their lives live with joy and hope in anticipation of being with God is one of the most convincing arguments to have a relationship with him. Nothing can take away this joy or hope!

Do you have the hope of a better future?

9

WHAT IS MY PURPOSE IN LIFE?

Not only do we need hope, we need a reason to live. We want to feel that our lives have significance. Because of this, we want an answer to the question "What gives my life meaning?" I have good news for you. When we discover it, we have what we've been learning about throughout this book. We have joy!

THE MEANING QUESTION

Once again, we've learned that we live for one of two feelings—happiness or joy. I want to get into these a little more.

Remember that happiness is a temporary feeling. It's often dependent on our circumstances. We can feel happy when we achieve some type of accomplishment, purchase something we've been wanting, have a physical experience that leads to some type of euphoria, get a raise or promotion…the list goes on. Our purpose is to get what makes us happy.

What happens when the happiness wears off? We're looking for something new to give us this feeling again. Brad Pitt, the famous actor, knows what this is like. He was interviewed in Rolling Stone magazine about his role in the movie Fight Club. The movie is about a man called Tyler who lives looking for satisfaction. Pitt said:

> *Tyler starts out in the movie saying, "Man, I know all these things are supposed to seem important to us—the car, the condo, our version of success—but if that's the case, why is the general feeling out there reflecting more impotence and isolation and desperation and loneliness?" If you ask me, I say, "Toss all this—we gotta find something else." Because*

all I know is at this point in time, we are heading for a dead end, a numbing of the soul, a complete atrophy of the spiritual being. And I don't want that.

The interviewer asked, "So if we're heading toward this kind of existential dead end in society, what do you think should happen?"
Pitt answered:

Hey, man, I don't have those answers yet. The emphasis now is on success and personal gain. I'm sitting in it, and I'm telling you, that's not it. …I'm the guy who's got everything. I know. But I'm telling you, once you've got everything, then you're just left with yourself. I've said it before and I'll say it again: it doesn't help you sleep any better, and you don't wake up any better because of it.[27]

There is another challenge. What happens when we face difficulties? These circumstances rob us of happiness. However, there are some who face them and continue to feel good about life. They maintain this positive feeling. How does this happen? They have a different pursuit.

They live for joy.

We've learned that joy can be never-ending. It's a good feeling of satisfaction that continues on. It's different from happiness. People with joy don't rely on their circumstances for happiness, they rely on a relationship with someone who has a love for them that never fails or disappoints. Their good feeling about life comes from knowing that nothing can take this relationship away. Their joy never ends because the relationship never ends. The relationship gives them their sense of identity. They are children of God. They experience joy because of the relationship and also when they help others have a relationship with the one they know. They have joy when others get what they have. In fact, it's their purpose to help as many people as possible get it. It's what gives their lives meaning as children of God.

Our feelings of happiness or joy indicate whether we are finding our meaning from the correct source—from circumstances or a relationship. Whichever we choose plays a role in forming who we are as people. Whatever we trust in to give our lives meaning gives us our identity. We've identified what we believe will satisfy us and we identify as one who believes in whatever or whomever it is.

With this in mind, what is your identity? What do you believe will give you satisfaction?

IDENTITY

The term *identity* was made popular through the work of a famous psychologist, Erik Erikson. He understood the important role that identity played in developing us into who we become, especially as these formations of ourselves take place within our youth. He made this evident in his book *Identity: Youth and Crisis*, written in 1968.

He wrote that identity was best described in a statement from a letter he had read, written by philosopher and psychologist William James to his wife:

> *"A man's character is discernible in the mental or moral attitude in which, when it came upon him, he felt himself most deeply and intensely active and alive. At such moments there is a voice inside which speaks and says: "This is the real me!"*[28]

From this statement, we understand that our identity is what makes us feel alive. It is what gives us a reason to live. It gives us a sense of purpose. It also results in a good feeling. We've learned that this feeling can be happiness or joy.

We want to feel alive. How do we? Where can we find this sense of well-being? Erikson went on to write that there are different elements that influence who we become. There are two factors: "…for we deal with a process *"located" in the core of the individual and yet also in the core of his communal culture, a process which establishes, in fact, the identity of those two identities."[29]*

What? What does that mean?

He believed our identity is determined by a combination of who we feel we should be and who our community tells us we should be. What happens because of this? We judge ourselves by what we believe others expect us to be and we judge others (the community) for expecting us to be like them when we desire to be someone different.[30] If we don't measure up to the expectations of a community, our identity can be in crisis.

What's the solution?

We either conform to the community's expectations or we change the community's expectations to conform to our own. Those who desire to live in a way that a society has determined to be unacceptable influence the culture to accept their way of life.

Our identity is defined in different ways. The expectations about who we should be can come in many different forms. Erikson taught that the traditional remnants of identity come from who we are economically, religiously, or politically.[31] He also wrote on the role that other identities play, including our sexuality. He understood that cultural changes in regard to these issues affect how we see our identity. This was understood in a real way during his own lifetime given the changes in social issues, gender expectations, and sexuality that were taking place during the 1960s.

One of the leading publications in the study of psychology, *Psychology Today*, speaks more to this:

> *"Identity encompasses the memories, experiences, relationships, and values that create one's sense of self. This amalgamation creates a steady sense of who one is over time, even as new facets are developed and incorporated into one's identity.... Identity includes the many relationships people cultivate, such as their identity as a child, friend, partner, and parent. It involves external characteristics over which a person has little or no control, such as height, race, or socioeconomic class. Identity also encompasses political opinions, moral attitudes, and religious beliefs, all of which guide the choices one makes on a daily basis."* [32]

The article shares the role that identity plays in everyday life: *"Identity encompasses <u>the values people hold,</u> which dictate the choices they make."* In other words, our identity is formed by what or who we value the most, and our identity influences our decisions.

Some deeply want others to approve of who they are and their way of life. Their motivation is to please the community. Others deeply want to be who they feel they are even though they know the community does not approve.

The article expresses how these desires can affect us: People who are overly concerned with the impression they make, or who feel a core aspect of themselves, such as <u>gender</u> or <u>sexuality</u>, is not being expressed, can struggle acutely with their identity. Reflecting on the discrepancy between who one is and who one wants to be can be a powerful catalyst for change.[33]

There is a key statement here. It's the discrepancy between who one is and who one wants to be. We can think of it as the difference between who we were created to be, and who we want to be.

There are those who don't want to be who they were created to be. This condition could also be defined as an identity crisis. This can especially be true regarding our sexuality. It may now make more sense why I spent so much time on sexuality while answering the Morality Question. It's a big part of who we are as people.

A decision is made by the individual as to who they want to be. We answer the questions "Will I be who I want to be?" or "Will I be who someone else wants me to be?" That "someone else" can be God. I can be in conflict when I desire to be someone that God did not create me to be. This crisis is solved in one of three ways.

THE OPTIONS

Option One: I exclude who God created me to be and wants me to be and I become who I want to be separate from him, believing that I know what is best for myself.

Option Two: I understand that I have a desire to be someone whom God did not create or wants me to be, but I believe that God knows and wants what is best for me, leading me to work to shift my desire to please him. I do this rather than please myself separate from him.

Option Three: I include God in my life, but only in areas where I agree with him.

The last of these options leads to a question. If I include God in my life, but only in areas where I agree with him, can he really be my God?

To answer this, we need to understand who or what a "god" is. Let's look at a simple definition: "God is any deified person, object or activity."[34] To comprehend the meaning of this definition, we need to define another term. What is a deity? "A deity is a person, thing or activity that is revered."[35] If it's revered, it's valuable to us. We respect the position of importance that it holds to us. We can put these definitions together to formulate a more comprehensive definition of God: a person, object or activity that we value the most and that is placed in the position of highest importance.

Our "god" is a part of our identity. Why? Our identity is determined by who or what we value the most. This is our god. It can be a little g "gods" or the big G "God." The little g "gods" are things in the world that we make most valuable and the big G "God" is the one who created us. This person or thing becomes the defining element of who we are.

I'll give you a personal example. I am a husband, a father, a son, and a sailor. There are many other words that could describe who I am. One of these descriptions of who I am is most important to me. Let's imagine that my being a sailor is most important. It's what I value the most, and I place it in the position of highest importance. This means when I have a choice to make about spending time with my wife, providing for my kids, or doing something with my dad, I'll choose to go sailing or go shopping to buy something to help me enjoy sailing. It's what I love the most, and because of this, I'll spend my time doing it and spend my money supporting it. It's my "god!" It's almost as if, when faced with a choice between sailing and something else, I ask, "What does sailing want me to do?" And another question goes with it: "Does sailing want what's best for me?"

If you were to name your "god," who would it be? Does your god give you everything you need in your life? We have certain desires. We determine if our god fulfills our desires. Let's consider some desires related to our identity.

MY DESIRES

- I desire to be protected, resulting in my wanting a solution to my problems.
- I desire significance. I want my life to matter.
- I desire to be loved, even when I don't deserve it.

With these in mind, we answer some personal god questions.

THE "GOD" QUESTIONS

- Does my god solve my problems? Remember, I need hope that my future will be better.
- Does my god give me a sense of significance by making me feel that what I do for my god matters?
- Does my god love me back even when I don't deserve it?

If my god doesn't meet my desires, I find myself in another identity crisis. I've identified with a god that isn't really what I'm looking for. Brad Pitt knew what this was like. It doesn't meet my desire for protection, significance, and love. If my god doesn't measure up, I feel a need to change. I search for a new identity. I look to trust in a new god.

We are all the same. The process of searching for our identity leads us to whomever or whatever has become our god. This same process has led many to find their identity in being a child of the God who created them. They have determined that he meets all of their desires.

They also believe he wants what's best for them. When we believe that the God who created us meets our desires and wants what's best for us, we'll make him our God. He becomes the one we value the most, and we place him in the position of highest importance. We have faith in him that he is trustworthy and knows what is best for us.

How does this change us? No longer do we ask, "What does sailing want me to do?" We ask, "What does God want me to do?" What does God want me to do for my wife? What does God want me to do for my family? How does God want me to spend my money? How does God want me to treat my neighbors? How does God want me to treat my co-workers? How does God want me to treat my body? How does God want me to protect humanity?

Jesus gave us the answer. We are to do to others what we would have them do to us (Luke 6:31).

I choose my identity. Will I choose to be identified as a child of God first and then identify with other pursuits in life that are consistent with who he wants me to be? Let's think about the options again. We'll do it in question form.

Option One: Am I choosing to identify as someone that I want to be separate from God?

Option Two: Am I finding my identity in something other than God but know that it doesn't meet my desires and that I need to make God my god, prioritizing my life according to His desire for me, recognizing he knows what's best for me?

Option Three: Will I include God in my life, but only in areas where we agree? If this is the choice, he can't really be your God. There is something that is more important to you than him. Remember the rich guy who talked to Jesus about having eternal life. He walked away. His god was his wealth. Whatever this is, that's your god. It wouldn't make logical sense that God would want to have a relationship with us if we don't value our relationship with him the most.

If we choose to become a child of God, knowing him gives us significance. The relationship gives us purpose. We live to show His love to others in hopes that they come to know him and find JOY! That's my desire for you!

ANSWERING HUMANITY'S COMMON QUESTIONS ABOUT GOD

10

WHAT WILL I DECIDE?

Let's go way back to love, the story about the Epicureans, Stoics, and Paul again. After he shared the message, they responded in different ways to what he said.

When they heard about the resurrection of the dead, some of them sneered, but others said, "We want to hear you again on this subject." At that, Paul left the Council. Some of the people became followers of Paul and believed. Among them was Dionysius, a member of the Areopagus, also a woman named Damaris, and a number of others. (Acts 17:32–34)

There were three responses.

Some rejected him outright. To them, if they didn't see it, touch it, or experience it firsthand, they couldn't logically accept it. They sneered! They didn't have faith that what they were hearing about Jesus was true.

Some were considering it. They were willing to listen to more.

Some believed. They heard the evidence and in their guts they knew it was true. They decided to have a relationship with God and become his children.

You've read information about Jesus and why Christians believe we need him. Looking at these three choices, what is your response? If it's to believe, you can decide right now to have a new identity as a child of God by accepting what Jesus did for you. Remember, we do it through talking to God. We learned a prayer that we can speak to him to make this decision. Will you pray it and begin this new relationship with God? I want to help you! Think of God in your mind, say these words with your mouth, and believe them with your heart.

PRAYER OF ACCEPTANCE

Dear God, I ADMIT that I have sinned and ask for your forgiveness. I BELIEVE that Jesus died on the cross to take the punishment for my sins and was resurrected to provide a way for me to live forever with you in Heaven. I COMMIT to follow Jesus as the Lord of my life as I live to become like him. I pray this in Jesus' name. Amen.

If you prayed this prayer and believed what you said with your heart, you have just made the most important decision of your life. Congrats! You can be confident knowing that this decision will give you what you've been looking for.

I want to encourage you to do something. Tell someone that you've made this decision. If someone gave you this book, please tell them. They'll be thrilled for you! Our telling someone is evidence that we believe in the decision that we made.

It may be that you're still thinking about what to do. I also want to encourage you to do something. If someone gave you this book, talk to them about what you're thinking. That was the question that was asked at the beginning: "What are you thinking?" Tell them what is keeping you from making the decision. They want to know. They want to help you decide your path in life. They would love to tell you their story of why they became a child of God.

No matter what you decide, know this: YOU ARE LOVED! The person who gave you this book cares about you, and God cares about you. You matter and God continues to pursue a relationship with you. My hope is that you find what you're looking for!

END NOTES

CHAPTER 1

1. "How Many Americans Believe in God?," Gallup, June 24, 2022, https://news.gallup.com/poll/268205/americans-believe-god.aspx.

CHAPTER 2

2. "Our Founders," Voice of the Martyrs, undated article accessed March 16, 2025, https://www.persecution.com/founders; "The Voice of the Underground Church," Wurmbrand Foundation, undated article accessed March 16, 2025, https://www.wurmbrandfoundation.org/richardwurmbrand.
3. "Atheism Fails in Crisis," Preaching Today, undated article accessed March 16, 2025, https://www.preachingtoday.com/illustrations/2003/september/14594.html.

CHAPTER 3

4. Henley, Karyn, *Love Trumps Karma: Uncovering the Truth You Know You Know*, (United States: Child Sensitive Communication, LLC, 2005), 16.
5. Henley, 24.
6. Barrett, Susan Laura, *It's All in Your Head: A Guide to Understanding Your Brain and Boosting Your Brain Power* (United States: Free Spirit Pub., 1992), 72.
7. Barrett, 72.
8. Strobel, Lee, *The Case for Faith*, (United States: Zondervan, 2014) 43.
9. Strobel, 43.

10. Strobel, 33.
11. Strobel, 50.
12. Henly, 26–28.

CHAPTER 4

13. "Edwin Hubble," NASA, undated article accessed March 16, 2025, https://science.nasa.gov/people/edwin-hubble.
14. Hawking, Stephen and Mlodinow, Leonard, *The Grand Design*, (United States, Bantam Books, 2010), 13.
15. Quoted by Stephen Meyer in "The New Cosmology: Theistic Implications," Counterbalance, undated article accessed March 16, 2025, http://www.counterbalance.org/cosmcrea/meyer-frame.html.
16. Durbin, Bill, "A Scientist Caught Between Two Faiths," Christianity Today, August 6, 1982, https://www.christianitytoday.com/1982/08/scientist-caught-between-two-faiths.
17. Aczel, Amir, "Einstein's Lost Theory Describes a Universe Without a Big Bang," Discover, Mar 7, 2014, updated April 9, 2020, https://www.discovermagazine.com/the-sciences/einsteins-lost-theory-describes-a-universe-without-a-big-bang.

CHAPTER 5

18. Campbell, Kelly, Holderness, Nicole , Riggs, Matt, "Friendship Chemistry: An Examination of Underlying Factors," National Library of Medicine, Published in final edited form as: Soc Sci J. 2015 Feb 18;52(2):239–247. doi: 10.1016/j.soscij.2015.01.005, https://pmc.ncbi.nlm.nih.gov/articles/PMC4470381.

CHAPTER 6

19. Henly, 38–44.
20. "Buddhist Beliefs—Edexcel," Bitesize, undated article accessed March 17, 2025, https://www.bbc.co.uk/bitesize/guides/zf8g4qt/revision/9.
21. "Morality & Ethics in Islam," Why Islam, undated article accessed March 17, 2025, https://www.whyislam.org/morality-ethics-in-islam.
22. "Logos," Brittanica, September 30, 2024, https://www.britannica.com/topic/logos.

CHAPTER 7

23. Strobel, 255–273.

CHAPTER 8

24. Stern, Adam P, "Hope: Why it matters," Harvard Health Publishing, July 16, 2021, https://www.health.harvard.edu/blog/hope-why-it-matters-202107162547.
25. "Hope," Dictionary.com, undated article accessed March 17, 2025, https://www.dictionary.com/browse/hope.
26. Snyder, C. R., "Hope Theory: Rainbows in the Mind," Psychological Inquiry 13, no. 4 (2002): 249–75, http://www.jstor.org/stable/1448867.

CHAPTER 9

27. Heath, Chris, "The Unbearable Bradness of Being," Rolling Stone, October 28, 1999, as archived at https://www.bradpittpress.com/artint_99_rollingstone.php.

28. Erikson, Erik H., Identity: Youth and Crisis, (United Kingdom: W. W. Norton, 1968), 19.
29. Erikson, 22.
30. Erikson, 22–23.
31. Erikson, 31.
32. Identity," Psychology Today, undated article accessed March 17, 2025, https://www.psychologytoday.com/us/basics/identity.
33. "Identity," Psychology Today.
34. "God," Dictionary.com, undated article accessed March 17, 2025, https://www.dictionary.com/browse/God.
35. "Deity," Dictionary.com, undated article accessed March 17, 2025, https://www.dictionary.com/browse/deity.

www.ingramcontent.com/pod-product-compliance
Lightning Source LLC
LaVergne TN
LVHW041254080426
835510LV00009B/732